Reality Leadership 2.0

Reality Leadership 2.0

Real Leadership Stories Igniting Inspiration *for the* Leader In You

Dr. Adrian B. Johnson

©2024 All Rights Reserved. No portion of this book may be reproduced, stored in a retrieval system, or transmitted in any form or by any means -- electronic, mechanical, photocopy, recording, scanning, or other -- except for brief quotations in critical reviews or articles without the prior permission of the author.

Published by Game Changer Publishing

Paperback ISBN: 978-1-962656-56-6
Hardcover ISBN: 978-1-962656-57-3
Digital: ISBN: 978-1-962656-58-0

www.GameChangerPublishing.com

Tribute to Lee Roy and Emma Mae Johnson
Education Mattered

Before I delve into my leadership experiences and thoughts on leadership, it's crucial to acknowledge the profound influence of my parents, Lee Roy and Emma Mae Johnson, my mom and dad. They were not only pillars of our community but also dedicated individuals within the public school system where I grew up. It's challenging to encapsulate the extraordinary people my parents were in just a few words or paragraphs. However, I'd like to share the heartwarming story of how they met, a story they passed down to me.

Their love story began in Austin, Texas, where Mom was a student at Huston-Tillotson College, and my dad lived nearby. One fateful day, my dad's friend, who played in a band, realized he had forgotten his saxophone at the boarding house where they lived. He volunteered to retrieve the saxophone and deliver it to him at the club where they were performing that night.

As Dad walked past the college on his way to the boarding house, he noticed several girls standing together outside. Among them, my mom approached him and asked if he played in the band. Being quick on his feet, my dad responded affirmatively, even claiming to have played with the renowned Nat King Cole. He continued on his way into the building.

However, when he emerged from the boarding house with the saxophone, he found my mother waiting at the gate. She inquired once more, this time wanting to know if he truly played with Nat King Cole. Lee Roy, feeling a connection with her, admitted he had lied, confessing that he simply wanted a chance to go on a date with her. To his delight, she agreed to accompany him to the show that night.

They attended the concert together, and despite the initial fib, they had a wonderful time. Little did they know that this night marked the beginning of a lifelong journey together, a journey filled with love, commitment, and a legacy that would shape the person I am today.

They tied the knot, and upon my mother's college graduation in May of 1947, they relocated to her hometown. She embarked on her teaching career at the all-black school, while my dad received a job at the white school. At the white school, he served as a bus driver and took on the roles of custodian and maintenance worker. Their commitment to education and their respective roles in the school system would shape their lives and contribute to the legacy they left behind.

My mom, a distinguished educator in the Frost Independent School District, hailed from the farming community of Brushie Prairie. After her graduation from several all-black schools, she pursued higher education, becoming the first in her family to attend and graduate from college. Her dedication to education was evident when she received a job offer immediately upon completing her college studies.

Throughout her career, she made an indelible mark on her family, friends, and community. She served as an elementary school teacher in the public school system for numerous years, passionately dedicated to making a positive difference in the lives of her students until her well-deserved retirement.

My mom's commitment to her faith was unwavering, as she confessed her faith in Christ at an early age and remained an active member of Saints Delight United Methodist Church. Within the church, she held various roles, including musician, choir member, Sunday school teacher, church secretary, and historian, and she also served as a Lay speaker. In addition to her church activities, she was a devoted volunteer for the 4-H club and a member of the Heroines of Jericho.

My dad (Leroy) continues to be warmly remembered in the community where he lived and worked. His enduring legacy resonates with family, friends, the community, and every student who had the privilege of crossing his path during his tenure as a custodian, bus driver, and maintenance worker until his well-deserved retirement. Notably, my dad's dedication extended to his role as a volunteer scoreboard operator at all the football games, an incredible 50-year streak without missing a single home game, earning him recognition in a local newspaper article.

My father was an unwavering member of the Saints Delight United Methodist Church, where he devoted 55 years to teaching Sunday school. His commitment to faith extended beyond the church walls, as he served as a district delegate at numerous annual conferences of the United Methodist Church. Additionally, he held roles such as District Director of Lay Speaking and Chairperson of Religion and Race. His active involvement extended to organizations like Promise Keepers and the Navarro County Emmaus Community.

Dad and Mom only had one child, who you are about to meet, but their circle of influence extends far and wide with numerous family members and friends who can testify to their unwavering dedication to God, family, friends, and education.

The story of how my parents met is a heartwarming tale of love and connection. It's evident that their love story profoundly impacted my life and instilled important values within me. Their relationship serves as a testament to the power of honesty and genuine connection in forming meaningful relationships. Honoring and paying tribute to our parents, who have played a pivotal role in shaping our identities, is a beautiful and meaningful endeavor.

READ THIS FIRST

Just to say thanks for buying and reading my book, I would like to provide a way for you to connect with me, no strings attached!

Simply Scan the QR Code Here:

Reality Leadership 2.0

Real Leadership Stories Igniting
Inspiration *for the* Leader In You

Dr. Adrian B. Johnson

www.GameChangerPublishing.com

Foreword

Dr. Adolph Brown

I am beyond thrilled and deeply honored to have been given the opportunity to write the foreword for *Reality Leadership 2.0* by the incredible Dr. Adrian B. Johnson. This book is an absolute gem that ignites inspiration and sets the stage for leaders to truly shine.

Dr. Adrian's authentic leadership style is tried, tested, and proven, making him the perfect guide to navigate the mysteries of leadership. Through his words, he unveils the realities of real leadership, whether they are imagined or experienced, and provides us with practical examples that are both relevant and effective.

What sets this book apart is Dr. Adrian's unique approach. After each dose of practical strategies, he encourages us to take a moment for reflection. This allows us to internalize the lessons and truly understand how they can be applied in our own leadership journeys. With supporting stories and examples, he challenges us to tap into our inner leader and equips us with the necessary tools to bring it to life.

I wholeheartedly recommend *Reality Leadership 2.0* to anyone currently leading, aspiring to lead, or simply seeking to become the epitome of leadership excellence. Dr. Adrian's solution-focused, goal-oriented approach, combined with his consideration of all realities involved, imagined scenarios, and past experiences, sets this book apart from the rest.

This is not just a book you read once and put aside. It is a treasure trove of wisdom that you will revisit time and time again. With each read, you will uncover new gems and nuggets that will help your leadership evolve into a practiced lifestyle rather than a mere theory.

Thank you, Dr. Adrian, for sharing your invaluable insights and empowering leaders around the world. Your book is a true masterpiece that will undoubtedly leave a lasting impact on all who read it.

Iron sharpens iron, and with "Reality Leadership 2.0," we can all become stronger, more effective leaders.

With utmost gratitude,
Dr. Adolph "Doc" Brown III
Master Teacher, Clinical Psychologist, & TV Host of ABC's The Parent Test

Table of Contents

Introduction 1

Chapter 1 – The Foundation 9
    The Name 11
    The Trail 15
    The Tale of the Purple Hull Peas 18
    Halloween Night 24
    The Older White Man 27
    The Young Black Man 29
    The Country Boy 31
    Christopher 35

Chapter 2 – 12 Essential Leadership Traits 41
    Empathy 43
    Integrity 47
    Communication 49
    Courage 53
    Adaptive 57
    Servant-Leader 61
    Inspiring 65
    Self-awareness 68
    Humility 71
    Optimistic 75
    Authenticity 79
    Decisiveness 83

Chapter 3 – You Think You Can Lead? 89
    Real Leaders Capture the Room 93
    Real Leaders Command the Situation 96

Chapter 4 – Taking Command of the Situation 101

Chapter 5 – Newly Leaders 111
    Blinders..113
    Mentor..114
    Mountain Top Mentor 120

Chapter 6 – Buck Dynasty 129

Chapter 7 – Mentor and a Real Influencer 135

Chapter 8 – Survivor 143
    Work Ethic...145

Conclusion 153

Introduction

The best definition I've come across for leadership is a set of behaviors aimed at aligning collective decision-making within a group. Collective leadership, which replaces outdated top-down models, emphasizes collaboration to achieve organizational goals, implement strategic plans, and sustain an organization's renewal.

Leadership encompasses a vast body of literature, from books and textbooks to graduate courses and online resources, exploring various theories and practices. It's a topic dissected by motivational speakers, researchers, theologians, politicians, and more. However, few resources delve deeply into the day-to-day realities leaders encounter, such as mentoring, motivating, team development, relationship management, driving change, and problem-solving.

Leadership skills are not merely theoretical; they must be honed through real-life situations. To illustrate this point, let's consider two professions that demand both technical and leadership skills: pilots and doctors. These professionals spend countless hours training in simulators and real-world settings because they never know what challenges they may face in their roles. Examining the leadership qualities of pilots and doctors provides a solid foundation for understanding leadership.

Contrary to some beliefs, leadership skills are developed in real-life situations, not just in the classroom or boardroom. This concept forms the basis of this book, *Reality Leadership 2.0*. I aim to inspire leaders by sharing real experiences, both my own and those of others, and some that I have imagined or observed. I hope to provide a gritty, authentic portrayal of leadership that goes beyond titles and superficial leadership. We will explore everyday leadership scenarios, teaching not only leadership traits, concepts, and frameworks but also taking leaders into virtual or live leadership simulation programs.

Many current leaders struggle to navigate organizations during difficult times, leading to high turnover, burnout, a shortage of quality leaders, and early retirements. Factors like increasing violence, politicization of education, and the impact of COVID-19 have changed the leadership landscape. Effective time management is also a critical challenge for leaders, as it impacts their well-being and the organization's success.

Managing real situations during both good and difficult times is a critical aspect of effective leadership. The key is to maintain a balanced perspective and be prepared for unforeseen challenges. Here are some strategies to manage such situations:

1. **Stay Level-Headed:** Regardless of whether times are good or bad, it's essential not to get overly emotional. Avoid becoming too euphoric during good times or too despondent during difficult times. Maintain a steady demeanor to make rational decisions.

2. **Develop Resilience:** Resilience is the ability to bounce back from setbacks. Building personal and organizational resilience is crucial. This involves developing problem-solving skills, adaptability, and a growth mindset.

3. **Training and Simulation**: Rigorous training and simulations are invaluable tools for leaders. Just as the military, medical, and aviation industries use drills to prepare for various scenarios, leaders should

undergo training that simulates real-life challenges. This helps leaders become more adaptable and effective in handling unexpected situations.

4. **Scenario Planning:** Leaders can engage in scenario planning to prepare for potential challenges. This involves brainstorming different scenarios, both positive and negative, and developing strategies to address them. Having a plan makes it easier to respond when situations arise.

5. **Crisis Management:** Develop a crisis management plan that outlines roles, responsibilities, and communication protocols in case of emergencies. Regularly review and update this plan to ensure it remains relevant.

6. **Continuous Learning:** Leaders should embrace a commitment to continuous learning. Stay informed about industry trends, emerging technologies, and best practices. This knowledge will help leaders adapt to changing circumstances.

7. **Effective Communication:** Maintain open and transparent communication with team members during both good and difficult times. Effective communication fosters trust and allows for quick responses to challenges.

8. **Team Development:** Invest in building a strong and cohesive team. A well-functioning team can provide valuable support during difficult times and contribute to organizational success during good times.

9. **Monitor Trends:** Stay vigilant by monitoring trends in your industry and the broader environment. Being aware of potential disruptions or opportunities can help leaders make informed decisions.

10. **Self-Care:** Remember that effective leadership starts with self-care. Leaders must take care of their physical and mental well-being to maintain the resilience and stamina needed to navigate challenges.

In summary, the key to managing real situations during various times lies in rigorous training, planning, and a proactive approach to leadership. By preparing for the unexpected and maintaining a level-headed perspective, leaders can lead their organizations successfully through both good and difficult times.

Unfortunately, I see too many instances where we practice what I call the "avoidance theory." Some people have proclaimed that the avoidance theory has merit; however, in the area of leadership, I find that avoidance behavior leads to complacency, which, during a time when leadership is needed, makes you look disconnected from the situation and those that you're supposed to be leading.

The "avoidance theory" is a mindset that can hinder effective leadership, often leading to complacency and a disconnect from the situations and people one is meant to lead. Leadership requires active engagement, especially during challenging times when decisive action is essential.

Recently, I witnessed a bizarre chain of events that was creating a major negative impact on an organization. At one point in the spiral of events, I noticed quality staff were emotionally devastated, physically depleted, and mentally exhausted. Quality people were publicly announcing their intent to resign and leave the organization. This would have had tremendous setbacks to the mission at hand. This situation lasted for over four months before someone confronted the issue. In the end, the results put the organization in a better position than when the situation started.

The story I shared about witnessing a series of negative events within an organization, leading to emotional and physical exhaustion among quality staff, illustrates the potential consequences of avoiding issues. In such situations, a proactive approach is necessary to prevent further damage and address the underlying problems.

The Chinese proverb "Maybe so, maybe not. We Will See." reminds us of the uncertainty of outcomes and the importance of patience and adaptability in the face of challenges. It emphasizes that, even in difficult circumstances, solutions can emerge over time, often with unexpected benefits.

A farmer and his son had a beloved stallion who helped the family earn a living. One day, the horse ran away, and their neighbors exclaimed, "Your horse ran away." What terrible luck.

The farmer simply replied, "Maybe so, maybe not. We will see."

A few days later, the horse returned home, leading two wild mares back to the farm as well. The neighbors shouted out, "Your horse has returned and brought several horses home with him. What great luck."

Once again, the farmer replied, "Maybe so, maybe not. We will see."

Later that week, the farmer's son was trying to break one of the mares, and she threw him to the ground, breaking his leg. The neighbors cried out, "Your son broke his leg. What terrible luck."

The farmer replied once again, "Maybe so, maybe not. We will see."

A few weeks later, soldiers from the National Army marched through town, requiring all the able-bodied young men to leave immediately to join the Chinese army. The farmer's son wasn't taken because he was still recovering from his injury. After the Chinese military left, the neighbors shouted, "Your boy is spared. What tremendous luck."

To which the farmer replied, "Maybe so, maybe not," but with a smile, he said, "We will see."

The moral of this story is about the unpredictability of life and the wisdom of reserving judgment. It teaches us that events that may seem lucky or unlucky at the moment can have unforeseen consequences, and it's often wiser to withhold judgment until the full impact becomes clear. The farmer's attitude of "maybe so, maybe not; we will see" reflects a perspective of patience and acceptance of life's twists and turns.

The underlying moral of this story is clear: when we confront our fears with confidence and a proactive approach, we gain control over the outcome rather than leaving it to chance. Preferring competence over luck, I refuse to let fear dictate my actions. Instead, I choose to master my fears through the practice of situational leadership.

The solution lies in a concept akin to sports coaches using drills and scrimmages or the military's preparation with war game planning. However, it's crucial to acknowledge that plans often shift immediately upon implementation or due to changing circumstances. Every action triggers a reaction, and the key to success lies in adapting your leadership style to the specific moment you're facing.

In the news, I recently came across a report about an airline pilot's skillful emergency landing when the nose landing gear malfunctioned. The airline highlighted its rigorous training for handling various emergency scenarios, reassuring that none of the passengers were harmed. This raises a critical question: How well-prepared are leaders in school districts and companies to deal with unscripted, real-world situations?

While many organizations provide valuable leadership training that reflects the latest practices and trends, the challenge lies in translating this knowledge into effective action when confronted with unforeseen challenges. The ability to implement leadership skills in dynamic scenarios is of paramount importance.

I offer or recommend two types of training sessions tailored to the specific needs of organizations. First, there are situational leadership sessions that help aspiring leaders assess their suitability for leadership roles. Second, there's "rigorous" and effective executive coaching designed for customized scenarios. As for my qualifications to provide this training and coaching, I remain humble and leave it up to you to gauge from my attached resume. I won't dwell on my achievements but instead would like to introduce myself through foundational and informative stories, illustrating the importance of preparing individuals for the unpredictable and uncharted situations we all encounter in the real world.

In the following pages, I will recount several pivotal experiences from my life that laid the groundwork for the development of my character, personality, and passion, all of which have left a lasting imprint on my career. Additionally, I will use various scenarios from my personal journey to provide glimpses into how the timing of events played a significant role in shaping my career and ultimately honing my ability to lead and mentor others.

By the end of this book, I hope that you will have gained enough insight into my life to discern whether I was inherently born with leadership traits or whether I embarked on a journey of learning and acquiring these traits over time. Furthermore, I aspire for this book to serve as a mirror, reflecting back on your own experiences and helping you unlock the keys to elevate your own leadership capacity, especially in the challenging times we all face today.

As I look back, I've come to realize that leadership often begins in unforeseen situations that demand our guidance. So, let's begin this journey by delving into the moment of my birth.

CHAPTER 1

The Foundation

Life indeed has a beginning and an ending; the journey in between is defined by our choices, experiences, and the people we encounter. Reflecting on one's life and the impact of various factors, such as the people we're around and our experiences, is a profound exercise that reveals the roots of our character and leadership journey. As Malcolm Gladwell aptly puts it in his book *The Outliers*, timing plays a pivotal role in shaping our path. I look forward to sharing my stories, which serve as a testament to the opportunities, desires, character, and confidence that have shaped my identity and leadership journey. These real stories have not only laid the foundation of who I am but have also played an instrumental role in shaping my character through the lens of my life experiences.

When you choose to read my book, you're essentially extending an invitation for me to enter your mind, your home, or your workplace, sharing my thoughts and experiences with you. Understanding the person behind the words becomes crucial in the context of leadership, as it can be a rather solitary endeavor. Therefore, it's essential to grasp the core of one's leadership journey. To begin this journey, let me introduce myself through a few real stories that have shaped my character and propelled me toward becoming a leader.

R.E.A.L. TALK

❖ When you look at your foundation in life, what major events have shaped your life?

_____

_____

_____

The Name

This story is closely tied to the concept of timing, as Mr. Gladwell discusses. In August 1955, within the small rural Texas community of Frost, my father found himself in a unique situation. He was asked to drive the local football team and their coach to Dallas, Texas, to attend an exhibition game between the Detroit Lions and the Philadelphia Eagles at the Cotton Bowl.

While at the game, the coach approached my dad with a request. He needed to tend to some urgent matters and, along with his wife, planned to take a bus home. My dad readily agreed to drive the players back to Frost and promised the coach that he would ensure their safe return.

During the game, the players engaged in some friendly betting, with most of them passionately cheering for the Lions. In contrast, my dad was enthusiastically supporting the Eagles. As fate would have it, the Eagles emerged victorious, and this earned my dad a hamburger from the players.

Later that afternoon, my father fulfilled his promise, ensuring that all the football players were safely delivered either to the school where they were to be picked up or directly to their homes. This trip created a special bond between him and the students and staff at the school, a bond that had formed before integration and continues to exist in that community to this day.

A few weeks after this memorable journey, my dad found himself rushing my mother to the hospital as she was going into labor. After several hours of labor, around six o'clock in the morning, a nurse came and woke my father, saying, "You have a son. What would you like to name him?" In that critical moment, he recalled the name of the Philadelphia Eagles quarterback from the exhibition game in Dallas—Adrian Burk.

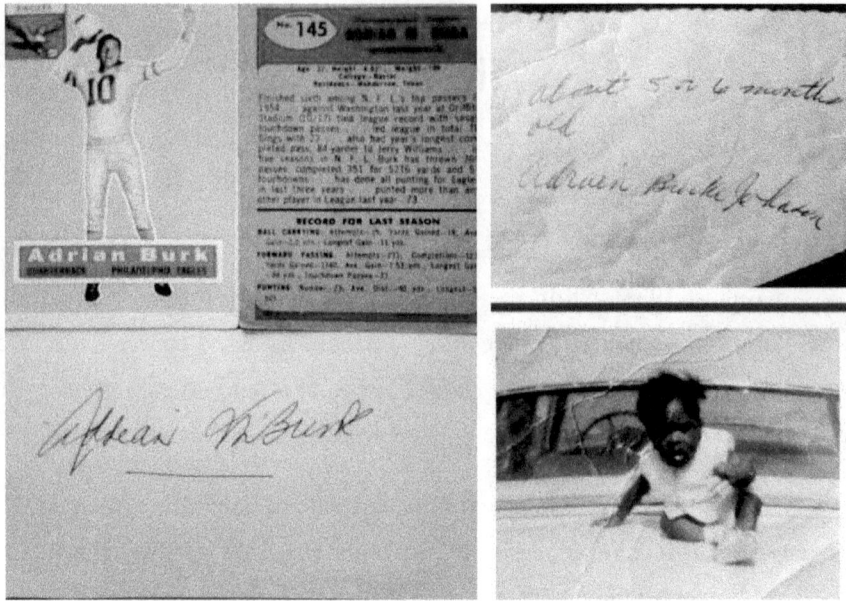

He instructed the nurse to name their son Adrian Burke Johnson. It's worth noting that the Philadelphia Eagles defeated the New York Giants on September 24, 1955, the very day I came into this world.

Years later, a dear friend of mine named Michael Donley presented me with a thoughtful birthday gift—an authentic football card from the legendary Adrian Burk, complete with his signature. Incidentally, Michael also recommended that I read Malcolm Gladwell's book, *The Outliers*, which delves into the profound role timing plays in our lives. This book thoroughly explored and analyzed how timing influences our experiences.

In our lives, so many positive and negative things transpire or fail due to the intricate dance of timing. Often, these moments shape the opportunities we encounter or the disappointments we face. The exhibition game and the unique connection my dad had with the coach and players occurred at a pivotal juncture in time, leading to the name I was born with and will carry throughout my life.

It's a reminder that we can never predict how a single experience at a particular moment in time might profoundly affect us in the future. The connections we make, the opportunities that arise, and the challenges we encounter are all intricately tied to timing. There may be other events stemming from this one that have influenced my life—perhaps yes, perhaps no. Only time will reveal the full scope of their impact.

R.E.A.L. TALK

- ❖ Did negative events ultimately have a positive influence? Did positive events ultimately have a negative influence? Maybe so, maybe not. We will see.

- ❖ What is your story?

- ❖ How has your story shaped your character?

❖ Where did your name come from?

_____

_____

_____

❖ How has the timing of an event impacted your life? Did you have any control over the timing, or did it just happen?

_____

_____

_____

★ *Reality: Given our inability to control time, it's wise to make the most of the time we have on this Earth, seizing every opportunity to create meaningful experiences and leave a positive impact on the world.*

The Trail

One of the formative experiences I've had, which has shaped my understanding of leadership, took place during my childhood in a quaint community called Brushie Prairie. The home where I grew up was nestled amidst sprawling farmland and towering trees.

One of my earliest and most cherished memories involves walking a trail that connected my house to my grandparents' residence. It was a magical experience, embarking on this journey to visit my grandparents, all while pondering questions like: Where did this trail come from? How did it come into existence? Who were the trailblazers responsible for crafting this path?

However, there came a day when I stepped out of my house, eager to visit my grandparents, only to discover that the trail had vanished. The crops in the fields had grown so high that I couldn't see the path anymore. I was lost without my guide, filled with trepidation about what I might encounter. In the end, I retreated to the comfort of my home, abandoning my quest to reach my grandparents. I frequently checked, but the trail remained elusive.

Then, one day, to my amazement, I noticed that the trail had reappeared. It was slightly different from the one I had traversed previously, but it led me precisely where I wanted to go—my grandparents' house. It didn't dawn on me at the time that various factors caused the trail to vanish intermittently, like rainfall, plowed fields, or the planting of new crops.

As I grew older, I gradually realized that it was my parents, grandparents, extended family, and friends were responsible for forging this trail. Through their daily lives and journeys, they left a trail for me to follow. I distinctly recall learning to drag my feet as I walked, ensuring that others could follow my trail. My cousins and I even ventured to create new trails to different parts of the countryside, discovering fresh opportunities and embarking on new adventures.

Over time, I can only surmise that some of these trails evolved into roads, roads expanded into highways, and highways became pathways that facilitated our journeys. I hope that by sharing my experiences and insights on leadership, I can contribute to creating a trail for future leaders, guiding them toward their desired destinations. Whether this trial proves valuable or not, only time will tell.

R.E.A.L. TALK

- ❖ Reflect on your personal trails.

_____

_____

_____

❖ Do you know where your trail is leading you?

❖ Are you on the path or trail to reach your destination or goals?

❖ Have you assisted others on their journey?

❖ Are you creating a trail for others to follow?

★ *Reality: What truly matters is not where you come from but whether you know your destination.*

The Tale of the Purple Hull Peas

In addition to his various roles within the school system, such as bus driver, maintenance worker, custodian, groundskeeper, and clock operator, my father was also deeply involved in farming. Our farm was a bustling hub where we raised cattle, chickens, and hogs while cultivating hay, corn, maize, and, notably, purple hull peas.

Among all the crops, my father was most renowned for his skill in growing purple hull peas. People from all corners of our community would flock to our fields to pick these peas fresh from the plants. The purple hull peas were the undisputed favorite, and there was something truly remarkable and inspiring about witnessing my father's relentless dedication. He would work tirelessly throughout the day and often into the late hours at school, only to come home and dive into the demanding tasks on the farm during the evenings and on Saturdays.

His work ethic was truly exceptional, and he belonged to a generation that exemplified a level of commitment and dedication far surpassing what we typically encounter today, including my own.

When I wasn't assisting my dad with farming duties, whether it was planting crops, hauling hay, or cutting firewood, you could reliably find me engrossed in the game of basketball. We even went so far as to pour a concrete slab and create a miniature basketball court on the side of our house. My passion for basketball eventually led me to opportunities at both the high school and collegiate levels.

During my time at Frost High School, I participated in a variety of sports, but it was evident that my greatest prowess lay in basketball. I was fortunate enough to secure an academic and athletic scholarship that allowed me to attend Navarro College in Corsicana, Texas, and play basketball there. My journey at Navarro began on a somewhat unexpected note. As a freshman, I made the team, albeit under somewhat unusual circumstances. If one player hadn't quit, and another hadn't had a mishap involving the dormitory stairs (for which I must clarify, I had no hand in), I might not have made the cut.

The competition for a spot on the team was fierce, with a roster filled with outstanding players hailing from various corners of the country, including New York, Indiana, Kentucky, Florida, and Ohio, as well as major Texas cities like Dallas and Houston. And then there was me, the country boy from Brushie Prairie, Texas, and a graduate of Frost High School. My teammates would affectionately tease me, suggesting that I hailed from the Ponderosa ranch, reminiscent of the Bonanza western show.

I must admit it was a challenging time for me. I grappled not only with my player status but also with the stark contrast in backgrounds, coming from a rural area amidst all these highly recruited players from diverse regions and bustling metropolitan areas. However, I turned to my parents for guidance during this period of uncertainty. They imparted a valuable lesson: "It's not where you are from that defines you; it's where you are going and whether you will reach your destination." They reminded me of our family's strong work ethic and encouraged me to apply it to my situation.

With newfound determination, I began dedicating extra hours to practicing and studying. I supplemented regular practices with rigorous workouts before and after, and even on weekends, all aimed at honing my skills and staying on top of my academics. I made a personal commitment and promised my parents that I would complete my college education. I refused to become one of those athletes who, once their playing days were over, never fulfilled their degree aspirations. Despite initially considering myself the 15th man on the roster, I persevered and earned my spot on the 15-member team.

I have vivid memories of the inaugural game of my collegiate career, a contest held at Hill College in Hillsboro, Texas, just a stone's throw away from my parents' residence and the very place I had grown up. My parents were bursting with excitement, eagerly anticipating my debut in a college basketball game. They occupied the first seats in the stands, enthusiastically sharing the news with everyone around them that their son had secured a spot on the Navarro Junior College basketball team.

Although I couldn't shake a slight tinge of disappointment, suspecting that they might not see me play unless the game took an unforeseen turn, I was determined to put on the best warm-up performance I could muster before stepping onto the court. As the game commenced, I found myself consigned to the end of the bench, quite literally at the farthest edge. It was a bittersweet moment, recognizing that, for the first time in my sports career, my parents wouldn't be there to witness my presence on the field or court at the start of a game.

Then, much to my amazement, while the game was still in the first quarter and a pause in play presented itself, Head Coach Johnny Underwood abruptly summoned my name as the first substitution. The players on the bench and even the starters on the floor displayed expressions of astonishment as Coach Underwood gestured for me to enter the game. Nervously, I shed my uniform and warm-ups, adjusted my shorts, and took to the court.

Everything unfolded in a whirlwind. As I moved in one direction, the teams were moving in another, leaving me feeling disoriented. My head was spinning, my heart racing, and I struggled to keep pace with the other players. Ultimately, I committed a foul, halting the play. At that point, Coach decided to remove me from the game after just a few minutes of play, and I didn't return. I've always believed that Coach Underwood's intention may have been to demonstrate to my parents, in his own way, why I wouldn't see much playing time. Following that debut, it seemed as though I spent more time watching basketball from the bench than actually playing it.

Captain, Adrian Johnson Frost

Nevertheless, over the subsequent year, I managed to earn more playing time and was fortunate enough to secure a full scholarship to play basketball at Tarleton State University in Stephenville, Texas. Prior to this opportunity, I hadn't even heard of the university, situated about an hour west of Fort Worth, Texas. Regardless, I was grateful for the scholarship that enabled me to complete my education while still indulging in the sport I cherished. I obtained my associate degree from Navarro College and set my sights on achieving a bachelor's degree at the university. My skills on the court continued to improve, and I even earned a place among the top 20 scorers in the Lone Star conference during my senior year.

R.E.A.L. TALK

- ❖ What kind of work ethic did you see in the people you were around when you were growing up?

  _____
  _____
  _____

- ❖ What kind of work ethic did you have growing up?

  _____
  _____
  _____

- ❖ How or were you involved in organized sports, activities, recreation, hobbies, or projects? How did they influence your character?

  _____
  _____
  _____

- ❖ Did you improve? Are you still doing it? Are you still good at it?

  _____
  _____
  _____

★ *Reality: At times in life, when contemplating surrender or abandonment, it can be beneficial to revisit your roots.*

Halloween Night

Traveling from my hometown of Brushie Prairie to Tarleton State University in Stephenville, Texas, during the 1970s presented a unique challenge. There were two routes to Stephenville, and several of them passed through small rural communities where, as an African-American, one might not always feel welcome. My parents and friends cautioned me to exercise caution when traversing these areas, which had developed an unfortunate reputation, whether deserved or not, for people of color. In essence, my parents strongly advised me to avoid stopping in these towns, as they might not be the safest places for someone who looked like me.

However, on the unforgettable night of Sunday, October 31, 1975, circumstances took an unexpected turn. I picked up another student on my way to Tarleton State, driving a sleek 1970 Gold Chevy Chevelle. We had just passed through one of these communities and were nearing a landmark area known as Chalk Mountain when my alternator light illuminated, signaling a loss of power in the car. I managed to steer the vehicle into a rest area on Chalk Mountain. Upon inspecting under the hood, it became evident that my alternator belt had snapped, leaving us stranded atop Chalk Mountain. Our options were limited—nine miles downhill to the town or 12 miles uphill over Chalk Mountain to reach Stephenville. Since cell phones were not a feature of the 1970s, we decided to embark on the descent down the mountain back to the small town we had just passed through.

Picture this scene: two African-American males, with toboggans on a chilly autumn evening, sporting afros, jackets, bell-bottom pants, and platform shoes, making their way on Halloween night down Chalk Mountain in the hopes of reaching the small town to find a pay phone and call a friend from Tarleton in the hope that they would come to our rescue.

Keep in mind that we were a couple of 20-year-old college juniors navigating the West Texas region, which had a notorious and historical reputation for being unfriendly to African-Americans. Our journey had just begun, and we hadn't walked very far when cars began to approach us, slowing down as if they might offer us a ride. However, as soon as the occupants caught sight of our appearance, they would accelerate and pass us by. I distinctly remember an 18-wheeler slowing down briefly until the driver saw us and then the unmistakable sound of the truck accelerating as it passed us by. It was at this point that we had walked exactly 4.5 miles, a detail I'll elaborate on later.

Suddenly, we heard the sound of barking hound dogs, and it became apparent that they were coming towards us, running through the weeds. It was too dark to see them, but we could clearly hear their approach as they moved through the underbrush, coming from the side of the road we were walking on. In response, I remember taking off my platform shoes and searching for rocks, preparing for a potential confrontation with the dogs.

However, our situation took a different turn when, out of the darkness, a porch light flickered to life in the distance, and a voice boomed out, "Hey, who's out there?"

My friend and I exchanged glances, and I made an effort to sound as non-threatening as possible. I called out, "Hey, we're a couple of college students from Tarleton State University up in Stephenville, Texas. Our car broke down on Chalk Mountain, and we're trying to get back to town to call some friends to come get us."

I must have sounded convincing enough because the man called off his dogs. Shortly after, we heard the rumble of a truck starting up, and its headlights pierced the darkness as it headed our way. By the time the truck pulled onto the road, I had managed to put my shoes back on, while my friend had initially taken off running but eventually returned upon my call. The driver was an older white man with a weathered appearance. I expressed my gratitude to him as he pulled up, offering us a ride. I attempted to get into the bed of the truck; he insisted that I climb into the middle seat next to him. My friend got in and closed the door, and we set off on our journey. I attempted to introduce myself and explain the car breakdown to the man, but he didn't seem particularly talkative.

Now, what I'd like to share with you is the account of this incident from three different perspectives.

The Older White Man

When he instructed us to get into the cab of the truck instead of the bed, I found it a bit unusual, but he was insistent. I glanced into the rearview mirror and soon understood why he had discouraged us from climbing into the back. There was another person in the truck bed, and that individual had a gun aimed in our direction. My immediate reaction was to shout, "Who's that back there?"

His response sent a shiver down my spine: "That's my protection in case you boys want to act up."

My friend, understandably terrified, began screaming and crying while I attempted to reason with the man. "Sir, all we need is a ride. You can simply pull over and let us out," I pleaded.

He chuckled and replied, "No, you boys should have never gotten in, and you damn sure should have never found yourselves stranded in this part of the country. Do you realize where you are? Your kind is not welcomed here, and we know how to deal with your kind."

He went on to express his appreciation for our arrival, stating that they hadn't had any "fun" with people like us in a while. He informed us that he was taking us to a Halloween party that some of his "friends" were hosting, claiming that our arrival would be a source of excitement for his buddies.

"My friends were already having a get-together tonight," he added, "and they'll be delighted that I brought you boys to the party."

At this point, he turned off the main road onto a gravel path. After a few miles, I could see a fire burning in the distance, with a crowd of people gathered around it. They compelled us to exit the truck, and the onlookers inquired, "Where did you get these boys from?"

He replied, "They claimed to be students on their way to Stephenville, but they broke down and came snooping around my house, probably going to rob me."

Without hesitation, they bound us, and the crowd subjected us to a brutal assault involving punches, kicks, and severe beatings that brought us perilously close to death. Thankfully, they did not take our lives and eventually transported us back to a store on the main highway, allowing us to call our friends to come to our rescue. We never reported this horrifying incident to any authorities, and I vowed never to drive through that town again.

The Young Black Man

As he directed us to get into the cab of the truck instead of the bed, I noticed that my friend, who was seated in the front, had discreetly produced a pistol, which he promptly pressed against the old man's temple, commanding him to pull over and step out of the vehicle. I couldn't conceal my shock and asked, "What are you doing? This man came out to help us and take us to the store to use the phone."

Ignoring my protests, my friend proceeded to clamber over the driver's seat, warning the old man that if he uttered a word to anyone, he would return to burn his house down and eliminate everyone inside. He informed the older white man that we were borrowing his truck for the night and leaving it on Chalk Mountain. We'd retrieve it the following day, but he better not report this incident to anyone. My friend proceeded to strike the old man with the gun and delivered a punch to his stomach, asking, "Do we have an understanding?"

The old man, clearly frightened and injured, managed to respond affirmatively, saying, "Yes, but I wanted to help you, gentlemen. You didn't have to take my truck and harm me."

My friend retorted, "Old man, I don't trust you or your kind, never have and never will. Do we have an understanding?"

The elderly gentleman, desperate for his safety, replied once more, "Yes, just please don't hurt me any further."

At that point, my friend confiscated the old man's wallet, extracted the cash, and instructed him to walk back to his house. We promptly departed, making our way back to my car. Utilizing a chain found in the truck, we towed my car to Stephenville, where we enlisted the assistance of some friends to return the old man's truck from Chalk Mountain. Surprisingly, we never received any attention from the authorities, and I made a personal vow never to drive through that small town again.

The Country Boy

When he suggested that we get into the cab of the truck instead of the bed, I expressed my gratitude for his assistance and mentioned that I hailed from a farming community and had grown up on a farm. The landscape around us reminded me of the farmland I knew so well. This shared connection sparked our conversation, and he inquired about the crops we grew. I listed off our varieties, including corn, hay, maize, black-eyed peas, and, notably, purple hull peas. His eyes lit up when I mentioned purple hull peas, and he exclaimed, "Man, I love purple hull peas!"

I shared stories about how people from all over our community would come to get my dad's fresh purple hull peas. I promised him that during the next crop season, I would bring him some of those delightful peas. He kindly took us back to the small town, where we were able to make our necessary phone calls, and he patiently stayed with us. Over nearly an hour, we swapped tales of farming, purple hull peas, hay hauling, and various other rural stories. As we finally parted ways, we expressed our heartfelt gratitude for his kindness in bringing us back to town and waiting with us until our ride arrived.

In these three scenarios, I've presented distinct versions of how the story could have unfolded, creating unique experiences that would profoundly influence one's attitude and character, both toward themselves and others. As it turns out, the final story involving purple hull peas is the true one. I remembered the distance we had walked—4.5 miles—because I would continue to measure it every time I passed through that small town during my college years. Regrettably, I never had the opportunity to fulfill my promise of delivering those purple hull peas, but I will forever cherish the memory of that kind-hearted man and his act of generosity.

I cannot fathom what might have been going through his mind and heart when he first encountered us and still offered us a ride to town. I don't know if anything I said may have altered his initial intentions. I can't say for certain if my composure helped my fellow students remain calm. What I do know is that in that one moment when I shared a bit of my background with someone from a different world, we found a connection that guided us through a potentially perilous situation. And the strongest connection of all was our shared love for purple hull peas.

A decade later, when I served as a high school principal at Hillsboro High School, our school district competed against the high school in that very community. I had the opportunity to get to know their administrators, particularly their high school principal, who was incredibly supportive of my efforts as an administrator. He even invited me to speak to his staff about diversity issues. I recounted this story to the staff powerfully and movingly, emphasizing that if we truly understand each other, we might discover more commonalities than differences.

During a break, one of his staff members approached me and revealed that she knew exactly who I was talking about; it turned out he was her relative. I was overjoyed but saddened when she informed me that he had passed away. I expressed how incredible that Halloween night had been and how I regretted not having the chance to thank him again by delivering those promised purple hull peas. She assured me that I was fortunate that night, and it reminded me of what my friend had said when I asked if I was good or lucky—he replied, "You were blessed. Blessed by God and purple hull peas."

I often wonder what might have transpired in those scenarios had I not mentioned purple hull peas. To this day, I don't just eat black-eyed peas on New Year's Day for good luck; I savor purple hull peas as well.

R.E.A.L. TALK

- ❖ Were there places in your life where you were encouraged or cautioned not to go there?

- ❖ Have you ever been stranded in life? Did someone help?

- ❖ Are the three scenarios believable or not? And why?

- ❖ Which scenario made you the angriest and why?

❖ Has a unique experience in your life helped you connect with someone else in a difficult situation?

_____

_____

_____

★ *Reality: We share far more in common with one another than differences when we simply take the time to share, listen, and learn.*

Christopher

In the summer of my junior year at Tarleton State University, I had the opportunity to work at Travis State School in Austin, Texas, where I discovered a profound passion for working with special needs students through an adaptive physical education and recreational program. The state school offered a variety of classes, including basketball, softball, track and field, swimming, and trampoline, among others. However, the most rewarding experience was coaching and participating in the Special Olympics Track and Field events, which took place at the prestigious University of Texas.

I volunteered as a "hugger" at the finish line during the Special Olympics. Regardless of a student athlete's finishing place, the time it took to cross the finish line, or their ranking, each participant received a warm hug and a blue ribbon. My time at the state school that summer deeply inspired me to pursue additional certification in special education. After graduating from Tarleton, I was determined to return to work at the state school in this special education capacity.

After graduating, I returned to the state school and was offered a position, although not in the physical education and recreational program I had previously worked in. Instead, I was assigned to work with non-ambulatory and non-verbal students who resided in a dormitory. The majority of these school-age children were confined to baby beds, and they suffered from various crippling diseases, including multiple sclerosis and muscular dystrophy, among others.

My first classroom was filled with students lying in these baby beds. My task was to take a toolkit and visit each bed, attempting to engage the students in stimulating activities and providing verbal and visual interaction. The passion I had developed during the previous 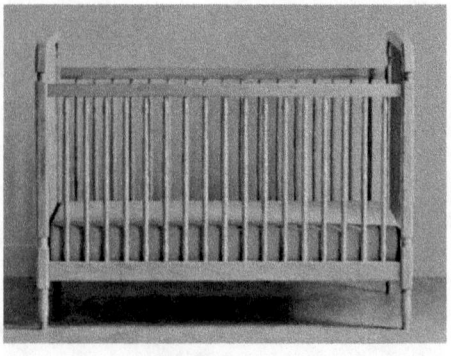 summer began to wane, and I felt increasingly frustrated each day as I struggled to connect with these children. I was on the verge of quitting, ready to give up, but then someone came to my aid.

At the end of my first frustrating week in this new role, I contemplated quitting and hoping for a position in the physical education department that I was more familiar with. During this time, my supervisor approached to observe me as I started working with a student named Christopher. Christopher was a 13-year-old boy who was non-ambulatory and non-verbal, suffering from a severe muscular disorder. He lived and learned while confined to his baby bed.

He observed me for a few minutes as I massaged Christopher's arms and legs and used a puppet to try to communicate and entertain him. However, I did not receive any responses from Christopher. Feeling exasperated, I turned to him and expressed my frustration, saying that I was using all my tools and training, but Christopher wasn't responding.

His response to me was unforgettable. He said, "You're only looking at what he can't do. You need to look at what he can do." With those words, he leaned over Christopher and began talking to him, asking a series of questions that assured me Christopher was responding, even though I couldn't see or hear it. He encouraged me to give it a try as well.

So, I leaned over to Christopher and asked, "Are you hungry?"

At first, there was no response. My supervisor admonished me again, emphasizing that I should focus on what Christopher could do, not what he couldn't. I tried once more, "Christopher, are you hungry?"

This time, I watched closely and noticed the little fingers on his right hand gradually opening. Curious if this was his way of communicating, I asked another question, "Christopher, are you ready to work?"

His fingers closed slowly. I continued, "Christopher, how do you say yes?"

His fingers opened gradually. "Christopher, how do you say no?" His fingers slowly closed. At that moment, Christopher smiled at me.

Christopher and my supervisor had imparted a profound lesson about life and learning. If a child like Christopher could find a reason to smile from his challenging position, then surely, we can find reasons to smile, no matter our circumstances. Moreover, as we teach and mentor children and adults, let us always begin the process with activities they can do.

R.E.A.L. TALK

❖ Have you ever looked forward to a new opportunity but ended up disappointed?

_____

_____

_____

- ❖ Did you quit?

  _____

  _____

- ❖ Did someone help you overcome your disappointment?

  _____

  _____

- ❖ Have you helped someone overcome their disappointment?

  _____

  _____

- ❖ Do you get frustrated when someone can't perform a simple task? How do you help them?

  _____

  _____

★ *Reality: Be willing to listen to others with more experience, realizing that when someone helps, a miracle can happen.*

These four stories of timely experiences in my early life have laid the foundation of some of the characteristics that have helped shape my life, career, and leadership opportunities. As I share my real administrative experiences, you will see where the timing, direction, relationships, and learning play a significant role in my ability to not only obtain leadership roles throughout my career but to truly be a leader ready for any situation.

CHAPTER 2

12 Essential Leadership Traits

At some point in your life, you may have heard someone proclaim, "I'm a born leader," or they referred to others as natural leaders. Perhaps someone even bestowed that label upon you. The truth, however, is that while each of us possesses certain personality traits that develop early in our childhood, leadership traits are not innate gifts handed to us at birth. They are acquired, honed, and practiced through life experiences and challenges.

The concept of trait leadership has a long history, with roots tracing back to researchers like Thomas Carlyle in the 1800s, who studied prominent leaders such as Gandhi, Abraham Lincoln, Napoleon, and Caesar. This theory suggests that leaders are born with specific inherent characteristics that distinguish them from followers. Some industries, like the military, have their own sets of leadership traits tailored to their unique requirements.

I firmly believe that leadership traits, whether inherited or developed, should play a pivotal role in leadership development and training. Leading others is not a one-size-fits-all process; it's more of an art. Strategies that prove effective in one organization may not yield the same results in another. This is because the variables, the people and environments—are in a constant state of flux.

This truth should serve as encouragement for aspiring leaders who are just beginning their journey. You don't have to possess all the knowledge and skills right from the start; it's an ongoing process that requires real-world situational leadership practice. Allow yourself the time to learn, make mistakes, and develop your leadership abilities.

While there are numerous valuable leadership traits, I'd like to emphasize the attributes that have significantly impacted my career spanning over 40 years. These attributes, while not exhaustive, offer a strong foundation upon which you can build your leadership journey. Let's delve into these twelve essential leadership traits:

Empathy

Empathy in Leadership has been studied for numerous years, and the evidence of its value and effectiveness is unchanging. When people feel heard, seen, and understood, they perform, are loyal, and trust their leadership to their best interests.

Empathy is defined in its simplest form: the ability to sense the emotions of others. As our world continues to recalibrate from the impact of COVID-19 and the injustice permeates every human system, empathy in leadership is critical to connecting with and relating to one's employees.

Theodore Roosevelt said, and I agree, "People don't care how much you know until they know how much you care." Real leadership cares.

"When people talk, listen completely," says Ernest Hemingway.

Empathy is a highly valuable leadership trait that involves understanding, sharing, and considering the feelings, perspectives, and needs of others. It plays a crucial role in effective leadership by fostering positive relationships, building trust, and creating a more supportive and inclusive work environment.

Here are some key aspects of empathy as a leadership trait:

- ❖ *Understanding Others*: Empathetic leaders take the time to understand their team members and colleagues truly. They listen actively and seek to comprehend the emotions, concerns, and motivations of those they work with.

- ❖ *Valuing Different Perspectives*: Empathy encourages leaders to appreciate diverse viewpoints and experiences. This can lead to more well-rounded decision-making and inclusive problem-solving.

- ❖ *Compassion*: Empathetic leaders demonstrate genuine care and concern for the well-being of their team members. They show empathy during difficult times and offer support when needed.

- ❖ *Communication*: Empathy enhances communication by making it more effective and compassionate. Leaders with empathy are skilled at delivering feedback and messages in a way that respects others' feelings.

- ❖ *Conflict Resolution*: Empathy can be instrumental in resolving conflicts. Leaders who empathize with the parties involved can help them find common ground and work toward mutually beneficial solutions.

- ❖ *Motivation and Inspiration*: Empathetic leaders can inspire and motivate their team members by recognizing their achievements and addressing their individual needs and aspirations.

- ❖ *Trust-Building*: Trust is a foundation of effective leadership, and empathy is a key factor in building trust. When team members feel understood and supported, they are more likely to trust their leaders.

- ❖ *Inclusivity*: Empathetic leaders create an inclusive and welcoming environment where everyone feels valued and respected, regardless of their background or differences.

- ❖ *Adaptability*: Leaders with empathy are adaptable and open to change. They can better understand how changes might affect their team members and help them navigate transitions more effectively.

- ❖ *Conflict Prevention*: By being attuned to the emotions and needs of team members, empathetic leaders can often identify and address issues before they escalate into conflicts.

- ❖ *Employee Well-being*: Empathetic leaders prioritize the well-being of their team members, recognizing that a healthy and happy workforce is more productive and engaged.

- ❖ *Long-Term Perspective*: Empathy helps leaders take a long-term view of their relationships and the impact of their decisions on individuals and the organization as a whole.

- ❖ *Customer and Stakeholder Relations*: Empathy isn't limited to internal interactions. Leaders who understand and empathize with the needs and concerns of customers and stakeholders can make more informed decisions and build stronger relationships.

In summary, empathy is a leadership trait that goes beyond simply understanding others; it involves genuinely caring about their well-being and considering their feelings and perspectives when making decisions and interacting with them. Leaders who cultivate empathy can foster a more positive and productive work environment while achieving better results through collaboration, trust, and effective communication.

R.E.A.L. TALK

_____

_____

_____

_____

_____

_____

_____

Integrity

Chapel of the Holy Cross

The need for integrity in leadership is as essential as breathing. Having strong moral principles and an unwavering commitment to truth, honesty, and ethical transparency are paramount leadership traits. I'm sure I don't have to belabor this point. We've seen how people respond to less-than-integral leadership. Our world suffered through a pandemic and, at the same time, grappled with the sad truth that our nation's leadership, blue and red, was sometimes ill-equipped and dishonest. The people's constant response to seek another leader validates the necessity of integrity in leadership.

Organizations have the desire to find integral leaders and develop integrity leadership traits in aspiring leaders.

Integrity refers to the quality of being honest, truthful, and having strong moral principles. It involves adhering to a set of ethical values and principles, even when no one is watching. Individuals with integrity are known for their honesty, reliability, and consistency in their actions and decisions.

Key aspects of integrity include:

- ❖ **Honesty**: Being truthful and straightforward in all dealings, not engaging in deception or falsehoods.

- ❖ **Trustworthiness**: Demonstrating reliability and dependability in commitments and promises so others can trust you.

- ❖ **Transparency**: Being open and transparent in your actions and decisions, not hiding information or motives.

- ❖ **Accountability**: Taking responsibility for your actions and owning up to mistakes when they occur.

- ❖ **Consistency**: Acting in alignment with your values and principles consistently over time.

- ❖ **Ethics**: Upholding a strong moral code and ethical standards, even when faced with difficult choices or temptations.

Integrity is a highly valued trait among individuals, organizations, and societies because it fosters trust, respect, and ethical behavior. It is often considered a fundamental element of good character and is essential for building strong relationships and maintaining a positive reputation.

R.E.A.L. TALK

_____

_____

_____

_____

Communication

Many of us learn the value of effective communication with the telephone game as children. Do you remember the telephone game? This is how to play the game:

1. Players stand or sit in a circle or a straight line. The idea is to be close enough to hear the phrase whispered by the person closest to you.

2. Starting the game, the person in the circle whispers the phrase to the person directly to their right.

3. The game continues until the last person in the circle or line receives the phrase.

4. The last player then shares the phrase with the group to see how much the phrase has changed since the first person spoke.

Although this is a considerably basic example, the lesson learned from the game points to the leaders' need to use effective communication to convey their thoughts, ideas, and provide direction. More importantly, choosing the proper communication channel cannot be overstated.

Communication is a critical leadership trait that plays a pivotal role in a leader's effectiveness and success. Effective communication is not just about conveying information; it involves the ability to connect with others, inspire them, and guide them toward common goals. Here are some key aspects of communication as a leadership trait:

- ❖ **Clarity**: A good leader communicates clearly and concisely. They can convey complex ideas in a way that everyone can understand. Ambiguity can lead to confusion and misunderstandings, which can hinder progress.

- ❖ **Active Listening**: Effective communication is a two-way process. Leaders must actively listen to their team members, colleagues, and stakeholders. This shows that their opinions and perspectives are valued.

- ❖ **Empathy**: A great leader understands the emotions, needs, and concerns of their team members. They communicate in a way that acknowledges these feelings, fostering a more empathetic and supportive work environment.

- ❖ **Adaptability**: Different situations and audiences require different communication approaches. A skilled leader can adapt their communication style to suit the context and the people involved.

- ❖ **Inspiration**: Leaders often need to inspire and motivate their team to achieve common goals. This involves using persuasive and inspirational communication to rally people behind a shared vision.

- ❖ **Transparency**: Transparent communication builds trust. Leaders who are open and honest about challenges, goals, and decisions create a more trusting and collaborative work environment.

- ❖ **Conflict Resolution**: Conflicts can arise in any team or organization. A leader skilled in communication can effectively address and resolve conflicts, facilitating a more harmonious working environment.

- ❖ **Feedback**: Providing constructive feedback is an essential part of leadership. Leaders should be able to give feedback in a way that helps individuals grow and improve without demotivating them.

- ❖ **Delegation**: Leaders must communicate tasks, responsibilities, and expectations clearly when delegating. This ensures that everyone understands their roles and contributes effectively.

- ❖ **Vision Communication**: Leaders are often responsible for articulating a compelling vision for the future. They must convey this vision in a way that inspires commitment and action.

- ❖ **Crisis Communication**: During challenging times, leaders must communicate effectively to address concerns and maintain stability. Calm and reassuring communication is crucial in such situations.

- ❖ **Cultural Sensitivity**: In diverse environments, leaders should be sensitive to cultural differences and communicate in a way that respects and acknowledges these differences.

Effective communication is not a one-size-fits-all skill; it requires ongoing development and adaptation to various situations and audiences. Leaders who excel in communication can foster trust, collaboration, and a positive work culture, ultimately contributing to the success of their teams and organizations.

R.E.A.L. TALK

Courage

Congratulations to Dr. Adrain Johnson who was selected at tonight's Board Meeting as the new Superintendent of Hearne ISD!

I've encountered numerous soft-spoken leaders in my career, but none of them lacked courage. The measure of a great leader has never been about how far their voice travels but rather about delivering consistent results.

Theodore Roosevelt coined the phrase, "Speak gently and carry a big stick." Although this phrase relates to engaging war enemies, we can extract leadership traits that suggest placing greater weight on having the courage to take decisive action when necessary rather than hurling threats.

It takes courage to make tough decisions and to admit when you're wrong. Good leaders take ownership of their failed ideas and projects. They become better leaders through failure.

Courage is a fundamental leadership trait that enables individuals to take risks, confront challenges, and make difficult decisions in the face of uncertainty or adversity. It is an essential quality because leaders often find themselves in situations that require them to act decisively, even when the path forward is unclear or potentially fraught with resistance. Here are some key aspects of courage as a leadership trait:

- ❖ ***Taking Risks***: Courageous leaders are willing to take calculated risks in pursuit of their goals. They understand that progress often involves stepping outside of their comfort zones and making bold choices.

- ❖ ***Facing Uncertainty***: Leaders must often make decisions in situations where the outcome is uncertain. Courage allows them to move forward with confidence, even when there are no guarantees of success.

- ❖ ***Resilience***: Courageous leaders exhibit resilience in the face of setbacks or failures. They learn from their mistakes and setbacks, bounce back, and continue to pursue their objectives.

- ❖ ***Speaking Truth to Power***: Leaders with courage are unafraid to challenge the status quo, question the prevailing wisdom, or speak out against injustice or unethical behavior, even when doing so may be unpopular or come with personal risks.

- ❖ ***Decision-Making***: Courage is crucial in making tough decisions that impact the organization and its members. This may include making difficult personnel decisions or changing the strategic direction of the company.

- *Innovation and Change*: Courageous leaders promote innovation and embrace change. They encourage their teams to explore new ideas and adapt to evolving circumstances.

- *Ethical Leadership*: Upholding ethical standards often requires courage. Leaders must stand firm in their commitment to ethical behavior, even when faced with pressures to compromise on principles.

- *Taking Responsibility*: Courageous leaders take responsibility for their actions and the consequences of their decisions, whether they lead to success or failure.

- *Empowering Others*: Courageous leaders empower and support their team members to take risks and make decisions. They create an environment where others feel safe to express their ideas and take initiative.

- *Standing Up for Values*: Leaders with courage stand up for their values and the values of their organization. They ensure that the organization's actions align with its mission and principles.

- *Inspiration*: Courageous leaders inspire their teams by setting an example. When team members see their leaders facing challenges with courage, it motivates them to do the same.

- *Negotiation and Conflict Resolution*: Courageous leaders are adept at negotiating and resolving conflicts, even in challenging or contentious situations.

- *Long-Term Vision*: Courage often involves making decisions that benefit the organization's long-term vision, even if they may not yield immediate rewards.

Courageous leadership doesn't mean being fearless; rather, it means recognizing fear or uncertainty and taking action despite it. Courageous leaders set the tone for their teams and organizations, creating a culture of resilience, adaptability, and ethical behavior. They are willing to confront adversity and make the tough choices necessary to drive their organizations toward success.

R.E.A.L. TALK

_____

_____

_____

_____

_____

_____

_____

Adaptive

Adrain Johnson
Superintendent
Hearne Independent School District, Texas

I'm reminded of one of my favorite books on coping with change, *Who Moved My Cheese?*—great leaders are adaptive. As leaders move to new environments and new companies, assuming more responsibilities, they're conscious of remaining open to new ways of doing things. Sure, they know what works, but they solicit input from key leaders to help them adapt to the company norms.

Adaptive leadership is a leadership approach that focuses on the ability to adapt and respond effectively to changing circumstances, challenges, and environments. It's a crucial trait in today's rapidly evolving and complex world. Adaptive leaders are skilled at navigating uncertainty, fostering innovation, and guiding their teams and organizations through periods of transformation. Here are some key aspects of adaptive leadership as a leadership trait:

- ❖ ***Change Management***: Adaptive leaders excel in managing change by understanding that change is a constant and inevitable part of organizational life. They help their teams embrace change and navigate transitions smoothly.

- ❖ ***Learning Orientation***: Adaptive leaders have a strong commitment to continuous learning and personal growth. They encourage their team members to develop new skills and knowledge to stay relevant in evolving industries.

- ❖ ***Flexibility***: These leaders are flexible and open-minded. They can adjust their strategies and approaches based on new information, feedback, and changing circumstances.

- ❖ ***Innovation***: Adaptive leaders foster a culture of innovation within their organizations. They encourage creativity, experimentation, and the exploration of new ideas and solutions.

- ❖ ***Resilience***: These leaders exhibit resilience in the face of adversity. They can bounce back from setbacks and use failures as opportunities for growth and improvement.

- ❖ ***Embracing Complexity***: Adaptive leaders are comfortable dealing with complexity and ambiguity. They can make sense of intricate situations and help their teams do the same.

- ❖ ***Empathy***: Understanding the perspectives and concerns of team members is essential for adaptive leadership. Empathy helps leaders connect with their teams and respond to their needs effectively.

- ❖ ***Collaboration***: Adaptive leaders promote collaboration and teamwork, recognizing that diverse perspectives and skills are valuable assets in solving complex problems.

- ❖ ***Strategic Agility***: They possess the ability to adjust strategic plans and goals quickly when necessary, ensuring that the organization remains aligned with its mission and adapts to changing market conditions.

- ❖ ***Anticipating Trends***: Adaptive leaders are forward-thinking and can anticipate trends and potential challenges before they become major issues.

- ❖ ***Crisis Management***: During crises, adaptive leaders can maintain a sense of calm and guide their teams through adversity. They are adept at crisis management and can make swift decisions in high-pressure situations.

- ❖ ***Communication***: Effective communication is crucial for adaptive leadership. Leaders must convey the need for change, the rationale behind it, and the vision for the future in a way that inspires and motivates their teams.

- ❖ ***Transparency***: Transparent communication is essential for building trust during times of change. Adaptive leaders are open about the reasons for change and the potential impacts on the organization and its members.

- ❖ ***Feedback and Reflection***: Adaptive leaders actively seek feedback from their teams and reflect on their own performance and decisions to make continuous improvements.

Adaptive leadership is particularly valuable in industries and environments characterized by rapid technological advancements, market shifts, and evolving customer expectations. Leaders who embody this trait can help their organizations thrive in an ever-changing landscape by encouraging adaptability, innovation, and resilience at all levels of the organization.

R.E.A.L. TALK

_____

_____

_____

_____

_____

_____

Servant-Leader

Although the Bible bears accounts of the greatest servant leader, Robert Greenleaf modernized the phrase. We understand the term to mean one who considers the needs of others before their own. A highly valued attribute that sets apart the selfless from the self-absorbed.

Servant leadership is a leadership trait and style that places a strong emphasis on serving and prioritizing the needs of others, including team members and the broader organization, before one's own interests. This approach to leadership is characterized by humility, empathy, and a focus on fostering the personal and professional development of those being led. Here are some key aspects of servant leadership as a leadership trait:

- ❖ ***Empathy***: Servant leaders are highly empathetic, actively seeking to understand the feelings, perspectives, and needs of their team members. They genuinely care about the well-being of others.

- *Listening Skills*: Effective communication is a crucial component of servant leadership. Servant leaders are skilled listeners who value the input and ideas of their team members.

- *Humility*: Servant leaders are humble and don't prioritize their own ego or personal gain. They are willing to admit their mistakes and shortcomings and learn from them.

- *Selflessness*: This leadership style emphasizes selflessness. Servant leaders are more concerned with the success and growth of their team members than with their own achievements or recognition.

- *Supportive Leadership*: Servant leaders provide support, encouragement, and resources to help their team members excel in their roles and achieve their goals.

- *Empowerment*: They empower their team members by giving them autonomy and responsibility, allowing them to make decisions and contribute to the organization's success.

- *Vision*: Servant leaders often have a strong vision for their team or organization, but this vision is aligned with the collective aspirations and needs of the team. It is not imposed but developed collaboratively.

- *Servant Leadership is Service*: At its core, servant leadership is about serving others. Leaders in this style often see themselves as stewards of their team's success and the organization's mission.

- *Community Building*: Servant leaders work to build a sense of community within their teams. They foster a collaborative and inclusive environment where team members support each other.

- ❖ ***Ethical Behavior***: Servant leaders uphold high ethical standards and set an example of integrity for their team members.

- ❖ ***Long-Term Perspective***: Servant leaders take a long-term view, focusing on sustainable growth, both for individuals and the organization as a whole.

- ❖ ***Conflict Resolution***: They are skilled at resolving conflicts and disputes within their teams, seeking resolutions that are fair and equitable.

- ❖ ***Continuous Learning***: Servant leaders are committed to their own personal and professional growth and encourage the same for their team members.

- ❖ ***Trust Building***: Trust is a foundational element of servant leadership. By consistently putting the needs of others first and demonstrating integrity, servant leaders build trust within their teams.

- ❖ ***Responsibility and Accountability***: Despite their emphasis on serving others, servant leaders hold team members accountable for their responsibilities and actions.

Servant leadership is often associated with fostering a positive organizational culture, employee engagement, and long-term success. By prioritizing the growth and well-being of their team members, servant leaders can create a motivated and committed workforce that is more likely to achieve collective goals and contribute to the organization's success.

R.E.A.L. TALK

Inspiring

Adrain Johnson
Most Inspirational Basketball Player

We all want to be inspired, inspired to live more, give more, and be more who we desire to be. Our leaders inspire us to perform and create an increase in value for our teams and customers in the workplace.

Being inspiring is a highly effective leadership trait that can have a significant impact on motivating and mobilizing a team or organization toward a shared vision or common goals. Inspiring leaders have the ability to ignite enthusiasm, passion, and commitment in their team members. Here are some key aspects of being inspiring as a leadership trait:

- ❖ *Visionary*: Inspiring leaders have a clear and compelling vision for the future. They are able to articulate this vision in a way that resonates with their team members and captures their imagination.

- ❖ *Passion*: Inspiring leaders are passionate about their work and the mission of their organization. Their enthusiasm is contagious and can energize those around them.

- ❖ ***Effective Communication***: They excel in communication, using powerful and persuasive language to convey their vision and goals. They are adept at telling stories and using anecdotes to make their message relatable and memorable.

- ❖ ***Lead by Example***: Inspiring leaders lead by example. They embody the values and behaviors they expect from their team members, setting a high standard for others to follow.

- ❖ ***Positive Attitude***: They maintain a positive and optimistic attitude, even in the face of challenges. Their positivity can boost morale and motivate others during difficult times.

- ❖ ***Resilience***: Inspiring leaders demonstrate resilience and determination. They don't give up easily, which can inspire perseverance in their team members.

- ❖ ***Empowerment***: They empower their team members by giving them autonomy and trust to take ownership of their work. This autonomy fosters a sense of ownership and motivation.

- ❖ ***Recognition and Appreciation***: Inspiring leaders recognize and appreciate the efforts and achievements of their team members. This acknowledgment reinforces a sense of value and importance.

- ❖ ***Listening Skills***: Effective communication is a two-way street. Inspiring leaders are active listeners and open to feedback and ideas from their team.

- ❖ ***Adaptability***: They are adaptable and open to change, recognizing that the path to success may require adjustments along the way.

- ❖ ***Authenticity***: Inspiring leaders are authentic and genuine in their interactions. Team members can see and trust their sincerity.

- ❖ *Coach and Mentor*: They invest in the development of their team members, acting as coaches and mentors to help them grow and reach their potential.

- ❖ *Team Building*: Inspiring leaders build strong and cohesive teams. They encourage collaboration and create a sense of unity and purpose.

- ❖ *Risk-Taking*: They are willing to take calculated risks to achieve their vision and goals, inspiring a culture of innovation and boldness.

- ❖ *Charisma*: While not always necessary, some inspiring leaders possess charisma. This magnetic quality draws people to them and makes them highly influential.

- ❖ *Celebrating Success*: They celebrate achievements and milestones, reinforcing the sense of progress and accomplishment.

Being an inspiring leader can have a profound impact on team motivation, engagement, and overall performance. Inspiring leaders can rally their teams to overcome challenges, embrace change, and achieve ambitious goals, creating a positive and dynamic work environment.

R.E.A.L. TALK

_____

_____

_____

_____

_____

Self-awareness

Although the phrase sounds self-explanatory, the meaning is much deeper, particularly as it pertains to leadership. As leaders, you must have a keen understanding of what makes you tick, your personality, emotions, and desires. The more self-aware you are as a leader, the better you can relate to others and the better understanding you have of how others perceive you.

Self-awareness is the ability to recognize and understand one's own thoughts, feelings, behaviors, strengths, weaknesses, and motivations. It involves having a clear and honest perception of oneself, including an awareness of one's emotions and how they influence actions and decisions. Self-awareness is a fundamental aspect of emotional intelligence and personal development. Here are some key aspects of self-awareness:

- ❖ *Emotional Self-Awareness*: This aspect involves recognizing and understanding your own emotions as they arise. It means being able to identify and label your feelings accurately. For example, being able to differentiate between anger, sadness, and frustration.

- ❖ *Self-Reflective Awareness*: Self-aware individuals engage in self-reflection, regularly examining their thoughts, behaviors, and experiences. They ask themselves questions about why they do what they do and how their actions align with their values and goals.

- ❖ *Awareness of Strengths and Weaknesses*: Self-awareness includes an understanding of your strengths and weaknesses. Knowing where you excel and where you may need improvement allows for personal growth and better decision-making.

- ❖ *Motivations and Drivers*: Self-awareness also involves recognizing what motivates and drives you. Understanding your core values, passions, and goals can help guide your choices and actions.

- ❖ *Impact on Others*: Self-aware individuals are attuned to how their actions and behaviors affect others. They can empathize with the perspectives and feelings of those around them.

- ❖ *Openness to Feedback*: Being self-aware means being open to receiving feedback from others, even if it's critical or challenging. It involves a willingness to learn and grow based on the insights of others.

- ❖ *Consistency*: Self-awareness helps in maintaining consistency in actions and behaviors. It enables individuals to align their words and deeds with their values and principles.

- ❖ *Self-Regulation*: Understanding one's emotions and triggers is crucial for self-regulation. Self-awareness allows individuals to manage their emotions effectively and make more thoughtful choices in challenging situations.

- ❖ *Improved Decision-Making*: Self-awareness supports better decision-making by allowing individuals to consider their own biases, emotions, and motivations when evaluating options.

- ❖ *Conflict Resolution*: Self-awareness is valuable in resolving conflicts, as it helps individuals recognize their own contributions to conflicts and take responsibility for their actions.

- ❖ *Personal Growth and Development*: Self-awareness is a foundation for personal growth and development. It enables individuals to set meaningful goals and work toward becoming the best versions of themselves.

- ❖ *Enhanced Communication*: When individuals are self-aware, they can communicate more effectively because they can express their thoughts, feelings, and needs clearly and respectfully.

Developing self-awareness is an ongoing process that involves introspection, self-reflection, and sometimes seeking feedback from others. It can lead to improved relationships, emotional intelligence, and overall well-being. Cultivating self-awareness is a valuable skill for personal and professional growth and can contribute to more thoughtful and intentional decision-making in various aspects of life.

R.E.A.L. TALK

_____

_____

_____

_____

Humility

C. S. Lewis said, "Humility is not thinking less of yourself; it's thinking of yourself less." This quote sums up perfectly how leaders perceive humility. Humility in leadership is not weak leadership; it's people-centric leadership. Humility keeps us grounded and available to serve others. The ego is rooted in managing, not leading.

Humility is a valuable leadership trait that involves a modest and unpretentious attitude, a willingness to learn from others, and a recognition of one's limitations and imperfections. Humble leaders prioritize the needs and contributions of their team members over their own egos. They are open to feedback and personal growth. Here are some key aspects of humility as a leadership trait:

- ❖ *Self-Awareness*: Humble leaders have a clear and accurate understanding of themselves, including their strengths and weaknesses. They are aware of their limitations and are not afraid to admit when they don't have all the answers.

- ❖ *Openness to Feedback*: They actively seek feedback from others and are receptive to criticism and suggestions for improvement. They view feedback as an opportunity for growth.

- ❖ *Empathy*: Humble leaders are empathetic and considerate of the feelings and perspectives of others. They show genuine care and concern for the well-being of their team members.

- ❖ *Servant Leadership*: Humility often aligns with the principles of servant leadership, where leaders prioritize serving the needs of their team members and helping them succeed.

- ❖ *Collaboration*: Humble leaders promote a collaborative and inclusive work environment. They value the input and ideas of their team and foster a sense of unity and shared purpose.

- ❖ *Sharing Credit*: They are quick to acknowledge and celebrate the contributions and successes of their team members. They don't seek personal glory but rather shine a spotlight on others.

- ❖ *Admitting Mistakes*: Humble leaders readily admit when they make mistakes and take responsibility for their actions. They view mistakes as opportunities for learning and improvement.

- ❖ *Continuous Learning*: They have a thirst for knowledge and are committed to continuous learning and personal growth. They actively seek opportunities to expand their skills and knowledge.

- ❖ **Respect for Others**: Humble leaders treat all individuals, regardless of their position or background, with respect and dignity. They do not use their leadership role to assert superiority.

- ❖ **Humility in Success**: Even in moments of success, humble leaders remain grounded and avoid becoming arrogant or complacent. They recognize that success is often a result of collective effort.

- ❖ **Conflict Resolution**: Humble leaders are skilled at resolving conflicts and mediating disputes. They approach conflicts with a desire to find fair and mutually beneficial solutions.

- ❖ **Ethical Leadership**: They uphold high ethical standards and integrity, setting a positive example for their team members.

- ❖ **Leading by Example**: Humble leaders lead by example. They demonstrate the behaviors and attitudes they expect from their team members.

- ❖ **Trust Building**: Humility contributes to trust building within teams and organizations. Team members are more likely to trust leaders who are genuine and modest.

- ❖ **Long-Term Perspective**: Humble leaders take a long-term view, focusing on the sustainable success of their team or organization rather than short-term gains.

- ❖ **Inspiration**: Humble leaders can inspire and motivate their teams by demonstrating that success is not about personal recognition but about collective achievement.

Humble leadership is not about being weak or lacking confidence; rather, it involves a balanced and realistic assessment of oneself and a commitment to valuing and elevating others. It fosters trust, collaboration, and a positive organizational culture, ultimately contributing to the success of the team or organization.

R.E.A.L. TALK

_____

_____

_____

_____

_____

_____

Optimistic

Leading in difficult times–periods of conflict, disaster, and uncertainty requires an optimistic outlook. When your teams feel uncertain about their futures, as many did during the global pandemic, leaders must lead with optimism.

I'm not suggesting that you give false hope about a situation but that you empower your teams to create the outcome they desire through positive conversation and active participation in their recovery and well-being.

When COVID barged into our lives, local, state, national, and international leaders said on multiple occasions and various statements. The coronavirus will go away; the virus will never go away. It will disappear one day. The virus is a hoax. It will disappear like a miracle. The virus is more deadly than initially perceived. The virus is just like a common cold. You treat this like the flu. You should wear a mask. You don't need to wear a mask. Is this an example of optimism, appeasement, false hope, or political posturing?

Of course, no one wants to be the bearer of bad news, but giving conjured-up information can foster mistrust, hurting your credibility as a leader. In times of uncertainty, it's okay to say, "I don't know, but I'm committed to finding a solution for a team, our community, our state, our nation, our world."

Optimism is a leadership trait characterized by a positive and hopeful outlook on the future, even in the face of challenges and uncertainties. Optimistic leaders inspire and motivate their teams by fostering a belief in possibilities, resilience, and a can-do attitude. Here are some key aspects of optimism as a leadership trait:

- ❖ ***Positive Mindset***: Optimistic leaders maintain a positive and constructive attitude, which can influence the overall morale and motivation of their teams.

- ❖ ***Resilience***: They exhibit resilience in the face of setbacks and adversity. Optimistic leaders bounce back quickly from failures and setbacks, demonstrating that obstacles are temporary and can be overcome.

- ❖ ***Problem-Solving** Orientation*: Optimistic leaders are solution-oriented. They approach problems and challenges with the belief that there is a way to find a viable solution.

- ❖ ***Motivation***: Optimism is contagious. Leaders with an optimistic outlook can motivate and inspire their teams to tackle difficult tasks and pursue ambitious goals.

- ❖ ***Risk-Taking***: They are more willing to take calculated risks because they believe in the potential for positive outcomes. This willingness to take risks can lead to innovation and growth.

- ❖ ***Vision***: Optimistic leaders often have a compelling vision for the future. They can communicate this vision effectively and inspire others to work toward it.

- ❖ *Adaptability*: Optimistic leaders are adaptable and open to change. They view change as an opportunity for growth and improvement.

- ❖ *Conflict Resolution*: They are skilled at resolving conflicts and disputes, often with a focus on finding mutually beneficial solutions.

- ❖ *Communication*: Effective communication is a hallmark of optimistic leaders. They can convey their optimism and enthusiasm to their teams, making it easier for team members to buy into a shared vision.

- ❖ *Stress Management*: Optimistic leaders are typically better at managing stress because they maintain a perspective that helps them see challenges as temporary and manageable.

- ❖ *Employee Engagement*: Optimism can increase employee engagement and job satisfaction. When team members see their leaders as positive and optimistic, they are more likely to feel valued and motivated.

- ❖ *Crisis Management*: During crises and turbulent times, optimistic leaders can provide a sense of calm and hope. They help their teams navigate uncertainty and find opportunities for growth.

- ❖ *Building Confidence*: Optimistic leaders build the confidence of their team members. By expressing belief in their abilities, team members are more likely to believe in themselves.

- ❖ *Long-Term Perspective*: Optimistic leaders take a long-term view and focus on sustainable success rather than short-term gains.

- ❖ *Innovation*: Optimism fosters an environment where innovation can thrive. Leaders who believe in possibilities encourage their teams to explore new ideas and take creative risks.

❖ ***Self-Fulfilling Prophecy***: Optimistic leaders understand the power of self-fulfilling prophecies. Their belief in a positive outcome can contribute to making that outcome a reality.

Optimistic leadership can contribute to a positive organizational culture, increased team motivation, and improved overall performance. While it's important for leaders to be realistic and acknowledge challenges, maintaining an optimistic perspective can help teams overcome obstacles and achieve success.

R.E.A.L. TALK

_____

_____

_____

_____

_____

_____

_____

Authenticity

There's a viral Oscar Wilde quote, "Be yourself; everyone else is already taken." This quote encapsulates the essence of authenticity. It emphasizes the importance of simply being genuine, both with oneself and with others. In our modern, image-conscious world, we often present curated versions of ourselves, showing only our most polished aspects. However, in leadership, authenticity is indispensable for fostering trust and enhancing performance. Exceptional leaders don't shy away from vulnerability; in fact, it distinguishes them and sets them apart.

Authenticity is a leadership trait that involves being genuine, transparent, and true to oneself in all aspects of leadership and interpersonal interactions. Authentic leaders are trusted and respected because they are perceived as honest and real. Here are some key aspects of authenticity as a leadership trait:

- ❖ **Self-Awareness**: Authentic leaders have a deep understanding of their values, beliefs, strengths, and weaknesses. They are in touch with their own emotions and motivations.

- ❖ **Transparency**: Authentic leaders are open and transparent about their thoughts, feelings, and intentions. They don't hide their true selves or their decision-making processes.

- ❖ **Consistency**: They are consistent in their words and actions. Their behavior aligns with their values and principles, which helps build trust.

- ❖ **Honesty**: Authentic leaders are truthful and straightforward. They do not engage in deception, manipulation, or dishonesty.

- ❖ **Vulnerability**: They are willing to show vulnerability and admit when they don't have all the answers. This vulnerability can create deeper connections with team members.

- ❖ **Empathy**: Authentic leaders are empathetic and understand the feelings and perspectives of others. They genuinely care about the well-being of their team members.

- ❖ **Listening Skills**: Effective communication is a two-way process. Authentic leaders actively listen to their team members and consider their input and feedback.

- ❖ **Respect for Others**: They treat all individuals with respect and dignity, regardless of their position or background.

- ❖ **Adaptability**: Authentic leaders are adaptable and open to change. They are not rigid or dogmatic in their beliefs and can adjust their strategies when needed.

- ❖ ***Ethical Behavior***: They uphold high ethical standards and set an example of integrity for their team members.

- ❖ ***Lead by Example***: Authentic leaders lead by example. They demonstrate the behaviors and attitudes they expect from their team members.

- ❖ ***Trust Building***: Authenticity contributes to trust building within teams and organizations. Team members are more likely to trust leaders who are genuine and honest.

- ❖ ***Humility***: Authentic leaders are often humble. They don't seek personal glory or recognition but instead focus on the collective success of the team.

- ❖ ***Inclusive Leadership***: Authentic leaders foster inclusivity and diversity within their teams. They create an environment where all voices are heard and valued.

- ❖ ***Feedback and Growth***: They actively seek feedback from others, recognizing that self-improvement is an ongoing process.

- ❖ ***Positive Impact***: Authentic leaders aim to have a positive impact on their team members and the organization as a whole. They work toward making meaningful and lasting contributions.

Authentic leadership is highly valued because it fosters trust, promotes open communication, and creates a positive and ethical work culture. Authentic leaders are more likely to inspire and motivate their teams, as their genuineness and integrity are evident in their words and actions.

R.E.A.L. TALK

_____

_____

_____

_____

_____

_____

Decisiveness

Decisiveness in leadership is a valuable quality that reflects a leader's maturity. As John Donne wisely observed, "No man is an island unto himself." Being decisive doesn't imply making hasty decisions without gathering essential insights from key stakeholders and others within your organization. Decisive leaders, once they make a decision, stand firmly by their choices.

Decisiveness is a critical leadership trait that involves the ability to make clear, timely, and effective decisions, even in challenging or uncertain situations. Decisive leaders are known for their confidence in their choices and their willingness to take responsibility for the outcomes. Here are some key aspects of decisiveness as a leadership trait:

- ❖ *Clarity*: Decisive leaders have a clear understanding of the situation and the options available to them. They can distill complex information into a straightforward decision-making process.

- ❖ ***Confidence***: They exhibit confidence in their decision-making abilities. Their self-assuredness can inspire trust and reassurance among team members.

- ❖ ***Risk Management***: Decisive leaders are adept at weighing risks and benefits when making decisions. They consider potential consequences and make informed choices.

- ❖ ***Timeliness***: Decisiveness involves making decisions in a timely manner. Procrastination or indecision can lead to missed opportunities or exacerbated problems.

- ❖ ***Adaptability***: Decisive leaders are also adaptable. They can adjust their decisions if new information emerges or if the situation changes.

- ❖ ***Accountability***: Decisive leaders take responsibility for their decisions, whether they lead to success or failure. They don't shift blame onto others.

- ❖ ***Decisiveness in Crisis***: During crises or high-pressure situations, decisive leaders remain calm and make swift, rational decisions to address the issues at hand.

- ❖ ***Data-Driven***: They base their decisions on relevant data and information rather than solely relying on intuition or gut feelings.

- ❖ ***Communication***: Decisive leaders communicate their decisions clearly and effectively to their teams. They explain the rationale behind their choices and provide direction.

- ❖ ***Alignment with Goals***: Their decisions align with the organization's goals and values. They consider the long-term impact of their choices on the overall mission.

- ❖ **Conflict Resolution**: Decisive leaders can resolve conflicts and make tough choices when disputes arise within their teams or organizations.

- ❖ **Empowerment**: They empower their team members by involving them in the decision-making process when appropriate, making them feel valued and engaged.

- ❖ **Decisive Delegation**: Effective delegation is another aspect of decisiveness. Leaders must delegate tasks and responsibilities confidently, trusting team members to execute them.

- ❖ **Strategic Decision-Making**: Decisive leaders prioritize strategic decision-making. They focus on choices that will have the most significant impact on achieving organizational objectives.

- ❖ **Consistency**: Their decisions and actions are consistent over time, helping to build a sense of reliability and trust among team members.

- ❖ **Customer and Stakeholder** *Focus*: Decisive leaders consider the needs and expectations of customers, clients, and stakeholders when making decisions that impact them.

Decisiveness is a leadership trait that is highly valued in a variety of contexts. It enables leaders to steer their teams and organizations through challenges and opportunities with confidence and direction. While decisiveness is essential, it is also important for leaders to strike a balance by considering input from others and being open to feedback, especially in complex and multifaceted decision-making situations.

R.E.A.L. TALK

- ❖ Do you believe these leadership traits are important, and if so, why?

  _____

  _____

  _____

- ❖ How many of these leadership traits do you already have?

  _____

  _____

  _____

- ❖ Identify at least one leadership trait for enhancement.

  _____

  _____

  _____

- ❖ Identify at least one leadership trait that is your strongest.

  _____

  _____

  _____

★ *Reality: Effective leadership encompasses a combination of traits such as empathy, communication, authenticity, decisiveness, adaptability, and humility, which, when combined, enable leaders to inspire, guide, and empower their teams while fostering trust, growth, and positive organizational cultures.*

CHAPTER 3

You Think You Can Lead?
(Developing Executive Presence)

"The quality of a leader is reflected in the standards they set for themselves." — Ray Kroc

"A leader is one who knows the way, goes the way, and shows the way." — John C. Maxwell

So, you believe you can lead, do you? In today's world, leadership is more critical than ever. The global pandemic has sent shockwaves through our communities, leaving people searching for leaders who can offer empathy, guidance, and, most importantly, solutions.

In certain contexts, leadership is often romanticized, with many aspiring to leadership roles without fully grasping the sacrifices and commitments required. As you cultivate an executive presence, you'll not only gain confidence but also earn the trust of others—both those you lead and senior leadership.

What exactly is executive presence? To ensure clarity before we proceed, let's establish a precise understanding of this concept. The definition I find most fitting is comprehensive yet offers hope to both aspiring and experienced leaders. Executive presence is a soft skill that can be nurtured and developed. It encompasses the capability to instill and maintain confidence in others regarding your leadership abilities, your effectiveness in motivating, and your capacity to connect with individuals at all levels within an organization. It also involves your aptitude for making difficult decisions. Similar to other soft skills like strategic management, executive presence is honed through practical experience in day-to-day operations, meetings, planning, and various other facets of your work. Your leadership competencies are constantly assessed, confirmed, and critiqued in your interactions with customers and employees, underscoring the importance of ongoing practice and constructive feedback.

How do you develop executive presence?

Developing executive presence is a conscious practice of owning how you show up as a leader and interact with others. Here are a few ways to cultivate your executive presence.

- Model Good Leadership
- Cultivate Good communication
- Churn Your Network
- Connect to Learn
- Share your story
- Know your people
- Look the Part
- Be an Active Listener

As a leader, it's crucial to avoid adopting a one-size-fits-all, impersonal approach to your staff. Instead of relying solely on your positional authority, you should prioritize personal connections. Take the time to engage with each member of your team individually. Building meaningful and positive relationships while assessing their strengths, weaknesses, needs, and desires is an effective way to achieve this.

Furthermore, as leaders, it's essential to continually enhance your toolkit and help your team do the same. You should develop multiple strategies and approaches to address the daily challenges you and your team encounter. I recall a highly respected principal within her community and school staff. Her campus consistently outperformed others with similar demographics. She maintained low turnover rates and garnered respect from students, parents, and the community. The school consistently excelled in the state's accountability system.

However, during the initial days of each school year, her teachers, staff, and students weren't immediately immersed in academic work. Instead, they spent a significant portion of their time learning arrival and departure procedures under various scenarios they might face throughout the year. This extensive preparation, akin to learning how to safely land a plane on water in case of an emergency, instilled a sense of confidence in the team's ability to handle unexpected challenges. When your organization is well-equipped to address unforeseen obstacles, it becomes better prepared to perform at a higher level and increase productivity, driven by the confidence inspired by your leadership.

There is no one-size-fits-all approach to leadership, and leaders have a multitude of resources at their disposal to address the unique needs of their staff. Since each member of the staff is different, it's essential to employ a variety of leadership tools that facilitate genuine staff development and foster real growth. Leadership should be approached intentionally and purposefully, involving guidance and planning to ensure the organization's staff is well-equipped for success.

Throughout my career, I've encountered numerous leaders who possessed a commanding presence but appeared to lack certain facets of character, substance, and style. I refer to these leaders as "veneer leaders."

As Wayne Cordero aptly writes in his book, *The Divine Mentor*, we live in a world where appearances often outweigh reality, where image takes precedence over substance, and where perception trumps actuality. Veneer leadership may appear genuine, but it tends to be less effective and can become genuinely problematic when confronted with a real crisis.

As you actively cultivate your executive presence, your confidence will undoubtedly soar!

Real Leaders Capture the Room

"Leadership and learning are indispensable to each other."
— John F. Kennedy

A friend once made a striking observation about me. He commented on my remarkable ability to command the attention of any room I entered. He recounted a particular incident when I attended a chamber Christmas luncheon, noting how I effortlessly connected with almost every guest present. He observed that people were naturally drawn to my presence, and he even went as far as likening me to a rock star. This compliment has stayed with me and holds a special place in my heart.

In my executive coaching sessions, I often pose two fundamental questions to participants:

Do you believe you possess the capability to captivate a room?

Do you believe you have the ability to take charge of a situation?

These questions are important because we've all encountered individuals who can captivate a room or assume control of a situation. These individuals have a distinct presence that stands out. It's what some people refer to as the "IT" factor. Some possess it naturally, while others may need to work on developing it. It's interesting to note that appearances can be deceiving, and some people who seem to lack this quality might surprise us.

The larger question is, how can one cultivate and develop this skill? For instance, consider the hypothetical scenario of Chesley "Sully" Sullenberger attending the same Chamber Christmas Luncheon. Would he have been perceived as someone who could command or captivate the room?

Absolutely, you've highlighted a crucial aspect of leadership—the ability to lead by example and command respect through actions and character rather than seeking personal recognition. True leaders often emerge when they respond effectively to critical situations, demonstrating their leadership qualities in practice.

In times of adversity and challenge, whether it's leading an organization through a crisis or addressing complex social issues, the skills and qualities that define executive presence become even more essential. It's through these real-life leadership experiences, both the successes and the challenges, that individuals can truly develop and refine their executive presence, gaining the confidence and ability to lead with authenticity and effectiveness.

As leaders learn from these experiences and continue to grow, they not only enhance their own capabilities but also inspire and guide others to follow their example, creating a positive and impactful leadership culture within their organizations and communities.

R.E.A.L. TALK

- ❖ Do you believe you have the ability to command the room?

_____

_____

_____

- ❖ Are you a good listener? Being a good listener involves being attentive to what is being said.

_____

_____

_____

❖ Do you like to network? When you meet and greet people, do you show true interest in the conversation?

_____

_____

_____

❖ Do you look people in the eye when you talk to them? Do you see EVERYONE in the room?

_____

_____

_____

★ *Reality: Executive presence is crucial as it empowers a leader to confidently and effectively command any situation, inspiring trust and respect among their team and stakeholders.*

Real Leaders Command the Situation

Effective leadership is far from a passive quality; it demands deliberate cultivation through rigorous training and the nurturing of authentic character alongside pertinent experiences. Genuine leaders possess the capacity to take charge of any situation, whether it be during trying circumstances or moments of triumph. The crux of this ability rests in how leaders adeptly handle unexpected real-world situations and their preparations for diverse challenges, conflicts, safety issues, threats, and unforeseen events.

One fundamental principle is to maintain equilibrium in leadership, avoiding excessive highs or lows. In essence, it's about developing the capacity to "land the plane in water," metaphorically speaking. This requires a commitment to learning and preparation for handling the unexpected. Just as the medical profession and aviation industry use drill simulations to train professionals, leaders should similarly prepare for unforeseen circumstances. Special Forces, doctors, pilots, and astronauts all engage in rigorous training to confront the unknown and handle unexpected challenges.

In leadership, it's a mistake to embrace the avoidance theory, which can lead to complacency. Avoiding difficult situations or failing to prepare for the unexpected can disconnect leaders from the reality of their role. It's essential for leaders to confront their fears, demonstrate confidence in their decision-making processes, and maintain control of the outcome. Doing so builds credibility with their team and colleagues, reinforcing their position as true leaders who can command any situation.

I would rather be good than lucky, and I'm willing to train to prevent my fears from controlling me. I will control my fears through rigorous training, the practice of situational leadership, and the guidance of experienced mentors.

Psychologist Andy Morgan from Yale highlights two critical factors that contribute to developing mental toughness for surviving crises.

1. **Training**: He said Special Forces training creates the same fear that the world experiences and captures. The special training creates the same fear they would experience in capture, interrogation, and torture. The fear produced by these exercises causes the cortisol to spike about as much as a patient undergoing heart surgery at about 20 times a normal rate. A study cited in a Harvard Business Review article also found that stress produces a hormone called cortisol. Too much or too little cortisol released in response to a stressor can have negative insight and negative physiological consequences. Morgan's research has shown that those who successfully finished the training had elevated levels of another hormone called Neuropeptide Y, which is believed to be a natural relaxant. Morgan found that how we talk to ourselves about stress and strengthening situations influences our neurobiological response to it. Once you express fear to yourself, Oh, my God, you release more cortisol. When you say, I know what to do here, this turns into a positive response and produces more neuropeptides.

2. **Talk about childhood:** Especially any childhood memories about trauma. The Yale psychiatrist asked soldiers to fill out a questionnaire about childhood trauma. Among regular soldiers, people who reported trauma and abuse were more likely to be upset by survival tests during training. The situation was reversed among Special Forces. Those who grew up with trauma and abuse were more resilient. Morgan speculates that the story we tell ourselves about our stress, trauma, and abuse predicts our future. If we see

ourselves as the victim, we become more sensitive to future threats. If, however, we feel tougher because we survived it, we have the mental tolerance to survive anything life can throw at us. How to make it work for you is in David Brooks' excellent article, "The Age of Calling is Over." David Brooks discusses how our efforts to eliminate stress or hardship that a child might encounter have backfired. Our over-protection doesn't shelter people from fear. It makes them unprepared to deal with the fear that inevitably comes. Instead, train children to master hardships, endure suffering, and build something from the wreckage. Confront the Beast. There are a few times when the avoidance theories have merit, but as a general rule, we'll need to face the Beast at some point. The reason is simple. If we don't face our fears, they will control us. Trauma and abuse often require enormous mental resilience. But this doesn't mean we will need to take the Rambo approach and become warriors.

The era of conventional leadership should come to an end. We must elevate training and executive coaching to higher levels of rigor, mental toughness, and mastery of various situations. When I step into an organization, I want to be led by someone who is well-trained, akin to a pilot who knows how to land a plane on water or handle a landing without landing gear. Higher expectations lead to higher achievements. This reminds me of the concept known as the "law of the hammer," popularized by Abraham Maslow in 1966. He suggested that when all you have is a hammer, everything starts looking like a nail.

In leadership development, we must adopt methods similar to those used in other industries to identify individuals with the capacity to lead, especially during turbulent times. This is why training leaders through rigorous simulations are indispensable."

R.E.A.L. TALK

❖ Do you feel adequately trained to take command of situations in your workplace?

❖ What do you fear ever having to do as a leader?

❖ Have you planned for the unexpected situations that could occur in your organization?

❖ Have you ever experienced an urgent or emergency situation? How did you respond?

❖ Any childhood experiences that impact your fear or confidence today?

_____

_____

_____

★ *Reality: Rigorous training equips leaders with the essential skills and confidence needed to effectively command any given situation, fostering their ability to make informed decisions and inspire trust in their leadership.*

CHAPTER 4

Taking Command of the Situation
(A Real Leadership Experience of
Taking Command of the Situation)

They call me "COOL BREEZE!"

Background

In 2006, I was appointed as the Associate Commissioner of the Texas Education Agency, responsible for overseeing all district and charter schools in the state. During that time, a rural school district in Texas was entangled in a legal battle to prevent the busing of students to a neighboring district. Despite winning favorable rulings in lower courts, including the United States District Court for the Eastern District of Texas, the 5th Court of Appeals eventually overturned these decisions, allowing the busing practice to continue.

Eight years later, after leaving my position at the state agency, I was approached to become the interim superintendent of that same rural school district. Accepting the role and later becoming the superintendent, I came to realize that the arguments made by the rural school and the late William Wayne Justice, a judge for the Eastern District, were accurate. Over the course of a decade, the district had developed a negative reputation, faced financial challenges due to declining enrollment, and performed poorly in state accountability measures.

Nearly a decade after the initial ruling, the Texas Department of Education threatened to take drastic measures, including closing, taking over, or consolidating the district. The district was in dire straits after going through six superintendents and interim superintendents in five years. In August 2016, I began receiving communications from the state agency indicating their intent to implement sanctions, such as appointing a board of managers, appointing a superintendent, or considering consolidation. I pleaded with my former agency to allow me time to address the issues before implementing such harsh measures, but my requests fell on deaf ears.

Here's the Situation

Another minority-majority school district was on the verge of closure, following in the footsteps of four other districts with similar demographics that the state department had already shut down. In response, I promptly assembled a leadership team, worked closely with the Board President and elected board members, and collaborated with the district's legal firm to prepare a defense strategy for the district.

Taking "Commando" the Situation

In January 2017, during the extended Martin Luther King Jr. holiday weekend, my wife and I took a quick trip to Atlanta, Georgia, for a getaway. One of the places we visited was the MLK Center, including his home and church. Although I never had the opportunity to meet Dr. King, he has always been a source of inspiration, a hero, and a mentor for justice throughout my life. In my eyes, he was an incredible leader and orator during his relatively short time in this world.

As I walked through the MLK center, some of Dr. King's quotes resonated with the challenges I was facing in the rural school district. I had grown up hearing the words, "Injustice anywhere is a threat to justice everywhere." I discussed the situation with my wife, realizing that taking command of this situation could potentially cost me my job. It was a metaphorical hill I was willing to die on. I often tell my colleagues and friends that my life's bumper sticker would read, "I brake for injustice and the unjust." I was fully prepared for the path my faith had placed me on, but this trip to Atlanta fueled my motivation to a whole new level. I had conquered my fear of the potential consequences and was laser-focused on what we could achieve for the benefit of others. I was ready to defend against the closure and takeover of this school district.

The hearing was ultimately scheduled for May 17, 2017, and my district team, along with the school district's legal counsel, had dedicated tireless effort to prepare and defend our case. We invested countless long days and late nights in rigorous preparation for this critical hearing. It was not lost on us that, during my tenure at the agency, four other school districts with similar demographics had faced similar circumstances, and none had been granted reprieve. Here is a condensed excerpt from our appeal for the formal review, with redactions made to protect the privacy of the school districts involved:

> **Over the past decade, the TEA has repeatedly sought to disenfranchise voters in districts with large African-American student populations through the imposition of a board of managers or the closure of the local school district. Examples include the current action against Hearne ISD, as well as actions against ▇▇▇ ISD, La Marque ISD (closed), North Forest ISD (closed), ▇▇▇ ISD, and Kendelton ISD (closed). Our initial research shows that districts with large African-American populations are significantly more likely to be subject to TEA sanctions that disenfranchise African-American voters from**

local control of their school district, as compared to predominantly White districts.

The average student population of all Texas ISDs is 12% African-American. The average student population of districts subject to a board of managers or closure orders in the past decade is approximately three times higher. In addition, while the average student population of all Texas ISDs is 29% White, we estimate that the average student population of districts subject to a board of managers or closure is only 6% White. In short, African-American students and African-American communities are much more likely to be subject to sanctions by the TEA that effectively disenfranchise African-American voters from local control of their schools.

While the agency may suggest that this is simply a function of poor performance by such districts, the TEA's own data show that this is not the case. There are 39 public ISDs that were rated Improvement Required in 2016. Of those, three were predominantly African-American districts that were subject to the severe sanctions discussed above. 31 of the remaining 36 districts were not subject to such sanctions. Those districts had an average student population that was only 8% African-American, yet 42% were White. The data shows that poor-performing school districts are more likely to have a higher percentage of White students compared to the state average, whereas sanctions against school districts are much more likely to target schools with higher African-American populations. Simply put, the data indicates that, even among lower-performing districts, the TEA has a history of looking the other way when it comes to predominantly White districts while severely sanctioning predominantly African-American districts, thereby effectively disenfranchising African-American voters.

We believe that the agency's history of such treatment towards African-American communities in Texas, combined with the continuation of such treatment towards Hearne ISD, may give rise to violations of the Voting Rights Act and the U.S. Constitution. Recent case law regarding the Texas voter ID law and the Texas redistricting maps have made it clear that federal courts will critically assess state action that have discriminatory effects on minority communities and their voting rights. See Perez v. Abbott, Civ. A. No. 5:11-cv-00360 (W.D. Tex. March 3, 2017)

███ ISD, ███ ISD, and ███ ISD.

The intent behind providing this background on the challenges faced by minority school districts is not to seek the readers' support or opinions on these specific issues; it's simply to acknowledge the reality of the situation with an "It is what it is" perspective. The aim of sharing this context is to convey the emotional and professional significance of the upcoming meeting in my capacity as the leader of this organization. Although my Board President suggested I travel to Austin the night before the meeting, given the two-and-a-half-hour drive from Houston, I insisted on departing from my home on the morning of the meeting. Ever since my visit to the King Center in Atlanta, I had a vivid mental image of myself driving to Austin that morning while listening to various sermons by Dr. King, using them as a source of motivation to address this challenging situation.

Recognizing the critical importance of thorough pre-planning, I took all the necessary steps to get organized the night before the meeting. Our team diligently rehearsed the presentation several days ahead of time, investing countless hours with our legal team. Personally, I employed GPS to calculate driving time and find the optimal route, meticulously organized everything, and methodically checked off all the boxes of necessary preparations for my departure the next morning. To bolster my motivation during the drive, I even compiled a selection of Dr. King's sermons and speeches.

The following morning, I sprang into action as the alarm clock rang. However, as I pulled out of the driveway, I encountered an unexpected thick fog that had descended unnoticed. The fog seemed to worsen as I continued my journey. I soon noticed several vehicles, including cars, trucks, and 18-wheelers, pulled over on the side of the road, causing traffic to crawl. Despite the slower progress, I maintained confidence that the fog would eventually dissipate, thanks to the extra time I had wisely incorporated into my schedule.

Approximately 30 minutes into driving through the dense fog, I began to experience discomfort in my stomach. Gratefully, my route included a Buc-ee's, renowned for its exceptionally clean restrooms, so I made a hasty pit stop for relief. Resuming my journey after this unscheduled delay, I noticed the fog was starting to lift. However, about 20 minutes later, as I reached for my phone to check my navigation time, I realized it was missing. I recalled leaving it in the restroom stall at Buc-ee's. A detour of another 20 minutes back to Buc-ee's was necessary to retrieve my phone, which a kind soul had turned in to management. In spite of all my meticulous pre-planning, it became increasingly likely that I would be late.

Eventually, I arrived at the meeting, albeit late, with my team, and to my chagrin, I realized I had forgotten my cufflinks, hence the rolled-up sleeves. After a quick stop for prayer in the foyer, led by Mr. Weatherspoon, my Assistant Superintendent, we proceeded to the state department, only to discover that we had left important files at the attorney's office. My assistant promptly departed to retrieve them. In the hearing room, we exhibited unwavering confidence and fearlessness, impressing some objective observers, including an attorney and training consultant for one of the largest educational organizations in the state, Kay Douglas, who lauded our presentation as one of the best she had witnessed at the state level.

A week later, on May 24, 2017, we received a letter from the State Department confirming the success of our appeal. We were granted additional time to achieve academic and financial progress in the rural school district. Over the last seven years, this district has witnessed a significant improvement in perception, financial stability, and academic performance, achieving full accreditation. We successfully navigated through the fog and safely landed the plane. There's nothing more rewarding than a job well done under immense pressure and heat and feeling a refreshing "cool breeze" of accomplishment!

That was the pivotal moment when I embarked on a deeper reflection about leadership, spurred by my travel experience. It was the instant I came to understand that no matter how meticulously you plan or what strategies you devise for yourself or your organization, there remains a fundamental reality that one must always be primed to confront. This experience and its timing serve as a compelling illustration of how to effectively command the situation.

R.E.A.L. TALK

- ❖ Do you have a cause that you will take a stand for? Fill in the blank: I brake for:

_____

_____

_____

- ❖ Is there a part of history that you feel strongly about? Why? Do you feel motivated to act upon it?

  _____

  _____

  _____

- ❖ Do you have some historical or divine mentors in your life?

  _____

  _____

  _____

- ❖ Do you feel equipped to land the plane in the fog?

  _____

  _____

  _____

- ❖ Do you have experience of taking command of a situation?

  _____

  _____

  _____

❖ Do you have people around you who are smarter than you are? Do you surround yourself with intelligent people who want the organization to be successful?

_____

_____

_____

★ *Reality: A true leader demonstrates their commitment to justice by fearlessly taking a stance against injustice and unjust situations, inspiring positive change, and serving as a moral compass for others.*

CHAPTER 5

Newly Leaders

(Create Your Own Definition of Success)

"I cannot give you the formula for success, but I can give you the formula for failure, which is trying to please everyone, everybody."
— Herbert Bayard

Much like the TV show *Newlyweds*, where couples aim to match perfectly, leaders entering new roles must strive for a harmonious fit with their organizations to avoid ending up in "termination court," and just as newlyweds often try to please each other constantly, aspiring leaders should define their own success criteria before committing to an organization, akin to seeking counseling before marriage. The counseling I have for aspiring leaders looking for the right organization is to create your own definition of success. Crafting your own definition of success, unswayed by external influences, is a trait shared by countless accomplished individuals across various fields who have relied on their intuition, identified their passions, and pursued their goals with unwavering focus, akin to the blinders worn by horses to maintain concentration and prevent distraction from what lies ahead. This principle is especially relevant for new administrators who may become apprehensive when sidetracked by peripheral concerns rather than staying focused on their primary objectives.

In our busy lives, juggling family, work pressures, and financial responsibilities, it's common to have a natural inclination to please others. To find success both personally and professionally, it's essential to don those blinders, maintain a steadfast focus, and not allow distractions from people or situations to deter you from your goals. The key is to establish your unique definition of success, remain committed to it, and, as I often ask children about their aspirations, reflect on what they wanted to become when they were younger and how that translates into your present-day reality.

Blinders

I heard the story of a young man in Austin, Texas, who graduated from the University of Texas with a degree in history. His father was a lawyer, and his parents always encouraged him to get his law degree to make good money and start a family. That was a success for them. That may not have been a success for him because he decided he wanted to become a minister, counsel young adults in his local church, and travel around the globe as a missionary.

This story of a young man who defied societal and parental expectations by pursuing his passion despite pressures to follow a more traditional path illustrates the importance of crafting a personal definition of success. When you identify your true passion, there will inevitably be doubters and naysayers, often well-intentioned family and friends who may not comprehend the fervor you hold for fulfilling your dreams. In such cases, it becomes vital to reevaluate and redefine success on your terms, putting on those blinders to stay unwaveringly committed to your passion and vision, undistracted by external influencers.

Mentor

"Mentoring is a brain to pick, an ear to listen, and a push in the right direction." — John Crosby

Once you've clarified your vision and cleaned your environment, finding a mentor who aligns with your personal and professional aspirations becomes pivotal. A mentor should not only champion your goals but also provide support, friendship, and the occasional push when needed, serving as your accountability partner. Good mentors may be rare, but when you discover one, it's crucial to nurture that relationship and retain them for as long as possible. They become your guiding light, helping you navigate through complexities and discerning genuine opportunities from those that appear too good to be true. When selecting a mentor, aim for someone who has not only achieved the level of success you aspire to but also has substantial experience spanning various periods and societal conditions, ensuring their insights are both relevant and invaluable to your journey, whether it's entrepreneurship, work-life balance, or any other goal you pursue.

When transitioning from a new leader to an experienced one, it's crucial to look forward and identify someone who embodies the success you envision for yourself down the road. Once you've chosen a mentor, engage in open and meaningful discussions over lunch or any suitable setting to tap into their wealth of knowledge and experience. This is not the time to be reserved or hold back; it's an opportunity to build a fruitful and productive relationship.

Ensure that both you and your mentor have the time and commitment to help you achieve your goals. Avoid the temptation to hop from one mentor to another; give the relationship a chance to develop, focusing on finding someone whose expertise aligns with your objectives and goals.

Once you find the right fit, arrange for an organizational meeting to clarify roles and responsibilities and consider these key factors in establishing a successful mentor-mentee relationship.

- ➢ Identify the roles your mentor can play to help you achieve your goals.

    _____

    _____

    _____

- ➢ Establish realistic expectations for the relationship. No mentor will do everything for you, and they shouldn't. Mentors are meant to guide you. You are to do the acting once the plan is created. What are your expectations?

    _____

    _____

    _____

- ➢ Communicate on a regular basis. You can possibly start meeting weekly and then shift to monthly. Later on, keep a regular meeting date. Canceling a mentor or mentee meeting date is not an option. Their lives are just as important as yours, and their schedule is just as important as yours. When?

    _____

    _____

    _____

- Establish relationship boundaries. Find out when and how you should contact your mentor if you have a question that you need an immediate answer to. What were your findings? How?

  _____

  _____

  _____

  _____

- Be prepared for each meeting. Type up an agenda, refer back to previous conversations, and make sure that things have been done that were supposed to be completed. Prep schedule:

  _____

  _____

  _____

  _____

- Most importantly, be open and honest with your mentor. If you hold something critical back from them out of fear or embarrassment, then your mentor cannot give you the proper advice for your situation. What do you need help with?

  _____

  _____

  _____

  _____

- Tell your mentor when you have a question about something he or she said or if you disagree with a statement. It's okay to have that back-and-forth relationship with your mentor because you actually help to mentor him or her as well in their ability to be a good mentor. But do it in a respectful way. Questions?

  _____

  _____

  _____

- Do not get defensive if your mentor makes a criticism or if he or she is trying to provide advice. Just listen and take away what you can from the conversation. What criticism or advice do you hear? How can you turn those criticisms into strengths?

  _____

  _____

  _____

- Your mentor may not be a wizard in all areas of interest to you. He or she may direct you to contact another person for advice. This is a good thing. Your mentor knows his or her strengths and can redirect you elsewhere if needed for one area. What areas of interest do you share with your mentor?

  _____

  _____

  _____

R.E.A.L. TALK

❖ What is your definition of success?

_____

_____

_____

❖ What factors influenced your definition of success?

_____

_____

_____

❖ Is your definition of success connected to your passion?

_____

_____

_____

❖ How would wearing blinders affect you? Would they make your goal too narrow, or would you be more distracted by what's happening around you?

_____

_____

_____

❖ Are you ready to be a mentor, and are you ready to be mentored?

_____

_____

_____

★ *Reality: The mentor-mentee relationship is pivotal in nurturing leadership development, providing invaluable guidance, wisdom, and support essential for shaping future leaders.*

Mountain Top Mentor

Indeed, mentors can come from various backgrounds and age groups, and their impact on your life isn't solely determined by their age but rather by the wisdom and experiences they bring to the table. This highlights the importance of being open to mentorship opportunities from a diverse range of individuals who can offer valuable guidance and insights based on their unique journeys.

Now, let me introduce you to the "Mountain Top Mentor." Over the past four years, my wife and I have been active members of CyLife Church in Cypress, Texas, which places a strong emphasis on discipleship. Intrigued by this, I decided to engage in discipleship training, and I was fortunate to be personally mentored by none other than our head pastor, Bob Reed. Pastor Bob Reed is the same friend who introduced me to the idea of a book study centered on *The Divine Mentor* by Wayne Cordeiro.

The significance of having trustworthy mentors for different phases of your life cannot be overstated. Cordeiro delves into some of the most influential divine mentors in the Bible, including renowned biblical figures like King David, Jeremiah, Nehemiah, and Mary Magdalene, among others. My experience with discipleship has left a profound impact on both my personal and professional life. It marks the first time I've made a conscious effort to deepen my spiritual connection with church leaders and fellow members, as well as a more profound exploration of my faith.

I've actively participated in numerous men's study sessions and have aspirations of launching my own small group to foster even more discipleship growth.

During a recent summer break, my wife and I organized a trip to Sedona, Arizona, to fulfill our mother's long-standing wish to visit this picturesque destination. Having visited Sedona several times in the past, I decided that this trip would provide an ideal opportunity for some dedicated spiritual reading, writing, and connecting with the unique vortex experience that Sedona is renowned for.

Sedona is celebrated for its stunning Red Rock Mountains, as well as the phenomena known as Vortexes or Vortices that possess a profound spiritual presence. These Vortexes are considered special locations on Earth where energy flows into or out of the Earth's plane. Vortices are frequently associated with sacred sites across the globe, but in the case of Sedona, many believe that its Vortex energy is exceptionally potent, to the extent that you can physically sense it. Some even claim that this energy can catalyze significant spiritual growth, which was precisely what I had hoped to encounter.

After enjoying several wonderful days of sightseeing with my family, I decided to embark on a solo excursion during our trip to Sedona, Arizona. My plan was to go hiking on one of the many trails in Sedona, potentially find a special spot, and perhaps even experience a Vortex while dedicating time to spiritual reading, writing, and meditation. This marked my first time hiking in Sedona, so I opted for a trail no longer than three miles.

My adventure began with an ascent up a small mountain known as "The Summit." However, it didn't take long for me to realize that my fear of being alone on a mountain, especially at my age, could potentially lead to a disastrous situation.

As I neared the summit, I noticed steel cables lining the edge, serving as a protective measure to prevent hikers from slipping over the side, as a fall would entail tumbling hundreds of feet down the mountain. To add to my unease, I realized I was the sole hiker on the trail heading to the summit at that particular moment. Despite being only 20 or 30 yards from the top, my heart raced, and I was taking deep breaths; fear had overtaken my entire being. I tried to convince myself that I could simply take a selfie from this point and then descend the mountain, and no one would be the wiser. However, the only person who truly knew the difference was me.

Instead, I made the decision to retrace my steps and return to the lower level, which still offered a spectacular view and featured some comfortable red rock benches—ideal for scripture reading, writing, meditating, and resting. Yet, for some inexplicable reason, I felt an inner urge to confront my fears and complete the hike. This experience taught me the importance of setting goals, and even if they aren't achieved on the first attempt, they should remain on your list until you conquer them.

I scanned my surroundings and noticed another trail called the Airport Loop, which seemed to have several hikers on it. However, I quickly realized that this trail, positioned along the mountain's edge, posed its own set of risks. The path was slanted and not level, making it easy for someone to slip along the edge, potentially leading to a disastrous situation. Given these concerns, I decided to rule out the Airport Loop as my chosen trail.

Then, I stumbled upon the third trail. Unlike the others, this trail wasn't situated on the edge of the mountain, and it didn't require any safety cables to prevent falls. It bore a resemblance to the trails I mentioned earlier, the ones I used to walk on the farm where I grew up. I thanked God for leading me to this seemingly safe trail and prayed for  the confidence to complete it. This trail was only 0.6 miles in length and appeared much more level and secure without the proximity to the mountain's edge. It felt like the right choice for me.

However, I couldn't help but notice that I was the only one on this particular trail when I started my hike. I assumed this was because it was considered the easiest trail compared to The Summit or the Airport Loop. It didn't take long after I began my walk along this trail for two epiphanies to strike me.

My first epiphany struck as the trail gradually transformed into a steep and rugged uphill climb. The second epiphany came when I realized I was entirely alone on this trail, as far as my eyes could see. It occurred to me that I might be the only one on this trail because it could be the most challenging of the three. Despite the initial allure of this trail, my breathing became labored, and the high altitude began to affect my stamina. I kept pushing forward, driven by my determination to achieve this goal and conquer my fear.

However, doubts began to creep in, and I feared I might not be able to complete this trail. Failing to reach the spiritual Vortex or achieve my personal goal of reaching the mountain's summit felt like a looming possibility. Then, suddenly, I was startled by the presence of someone walking up behind me. I promptly stepped aside to let this young man pass.

He must have noticed my surprise and apologized for startling me. It was evident that he was familiar with the trail, and I observed that he was wearing sandals. I asked him about the distance to the top and explained that I believed I was close to halfway there. He responded politely, and without words, I could tell he was concerned about my well-being, likely due to my heavy breathing and demeanor. We began walking together for a while, continuing our ascent. He mentioned that he and his wife were traveling from Salt Lake City, Utah, and had been camping at various locations across the country. However, due to the heat, they decided to stay in a hotel in the Sedona area, which was on the other side of the hill. This explained his familiarity with the trail. He also shared his disappointment in not having experienced the Vortex on other trails.

We talked about the other two trails, The Summit and the Airport Loop, and discussed their challenges. It seemed that having someone to talk to, especially an experienced hiker, filled me with the confidence I needed to persevere. Additionally, it's harder to give in to fear when someone else is present. So, I knew I had to step up and continue. Having someone around can be a motivating factor in dealing with challenging situations. He informed me that we were nearing the top of the hill and that the final portion of the hike wouldn't be as steep. It wasn't long before he pointed out the perfect bench at the mountain's summit to complete my climb.

Then, my third epiphany struck, and it dawned on me that I had just conquered the mountain known as the "Scenic View," the very mountain my family had been hesitant to even drive up just two days ago. My new friend found this amusing, and he chuckled at the irony. He then noticed that I didn't have any water with me and scolded me gently, emphasizing that dehydration is a significant concern when hiking at this altitude, especially in the heat. He insisted I take his water thermos for my descent down the trail, a gesture I deeply appreciated.

Following his advice, I relaxed, savored the breathtaking view, took some photographs, and enjoyed our conversation. I expressed my gratitude for his guidance and assistance. Overwhelmed with a sense of accomplishment and pride for conquering my fears and achieving one of my goals, I felt like I had met a mountain mentor that day.

As we prepared to part ways, I extended my hand for a handshake and introduced myself, "My name is Adrian."

He responded, "I'm glad to meet you, Adrian. My name is David!"

Our parting thoughts led me to reflect on the significance of the name David, particularly King David, and the importance of having a mentor, whether in a divine, professional, or personal capacity. While he was likely half my age, his wealth of experience in hiking and climbing proved invaluable to me, complementing my own extensive leadership experience. It served as a reminder that we can all learn from one another when we position ourselves in the right place at the right time, foster meaningful relationships, and are open and honest about our needs and goals. Had I not engaged in conversation with him and approached him with positivity, he might not have become my mountain mentor.

In the end, I achieved my goal of conquering the uphill trail, thanks in no small part to the guidance of a knowledgeable mentor who had experience in the very area I sought to master. I couldn't help but believe that, at that moment, we had indeed experienced a Vortex in Sedona.

R.E.A.L. TALK

- ❖ What or where is your summit?

  _____

  _____

  _____

- ❖ Do you have a quality mentor(s) in your life?

  _____

  _____

  _____

- ❖ Does your mentor have some of the skills you want to develop?

  _____

  _____

  _____

- ❖ Are you good at building real relationships? Why or why not?

  _____

  _____

  _____

❖ Have you had a "Mountain Top Moment"? Did someone help you? Please share.

_____

_____

_____

★ *Reality: Achieving a mentally and physically intimidating goal signifies one's resilience, determination, and capacity to transcend personal limitations, serving as a testament to the power of the human spirit.*

CHAPTER 6

Buck Dynasty

"You don't hold your own in the world by standing on guard, but by attacking and getting well hammered yourself." — George Bernard Shaw

How can you make significant progress in pursuing your passion and achieving your goals? One effective strategy is to create a "success to-do list" and prominently display it where you can see it daily. This approach serves as a constant source of motivation and a clear roadmap toward your aspirations. By having a tangible list, you can stay organized and maintain your focus on the path to success, making your objectives seem more achievable. Regularly reviewing this list reinforces your commitment and determination, bringing you closer to realizing your dreams.

For example, if your ambition is to start your own business, consider enrolling in courses that specialize in small business management. Additionally, improving your credit score by settling any outstanding credit card debts can lead to more favorable interest rates when seeking a small business loan. On the other hand, if your passion is in politics and you aspire to run for public office, take proactive steps such as dedicating your weekends to work on political campaigns, getting involved with local boards, or volunteering in the office of a public official. If you want to become a billionaire, then hire me! Identify the specific skills to acquire, the obstacles to overcome, and the connections to establish to reach your goals.

Document these crucial elements on your "success to-do list." Personally, I keep mine on my iPhone, ensuring that every day, while managing my routine, I can review and maintain my focus on my top priorities.

When mentoring individuals, I often emphasize the importance of "keeping the main thing the main thing." Take a moment to review your list and ensure that every item listed contributes in some manner to your overarching goal. This list serves as a daily reminder of the steps required to reach your destination. However, it's essential not to overwhelm yourself with this list; it can evolve and adapt over time. I understand that some high achievers may be reading this and thinking that accomplishing objectives like paying off credit card debt, earning a college degree, working full-time, and being an excellent parent within a mere two years is an insurmountable challenge. To them, I say, "Stop stressing." That's not the purpose of the list. The top 10 list isn't meant to induce stress. Rather, it's a tool to help you maintain focus and make informed choices as you navigate through the various experiences that life presents. Life is defined by the choices we make, and your top ten list will assist you in making choices that align with your overarching plan.

Now, how do you make strides in fulfilling your passion and leading an organization to accomplish its goals? Familiarize yourself with good planning models, both strategic.

To significantly advance in pursuing your passion and lead an organization effectively toward achieving its goals, it is crucial to become proficient in effective planning models, including both strategic and operational. Strategic planning focuses on determining where you want to go, while operational planning outlines how you will get there.

Here's an example from my own experience: Imagine an organization that was on the brink of collapse, facing an inevitable takeover, a scenario no one desired. To address this, we convened the entire executive team in a room and started with a clean slate—a blank whiteboard. We began by establishing realistic and achievable goals and creating a feasible timeline. We recognized the need for expert guidance and decided to form a board of advisors (mentors) from highly successful organizations in our region and state. Their insights would be invaluable in shaping our action plan.

We also sought to bring in individuals with relevant experiences and success stories in areas where our organization had weaknesses. Our approach included intensive training, strategic and operational planning, the implementation of SMART (Specific, Measurable, Achievable, Relevant, and Time-Bound) goals, and the adoption of the Improvement Science model. Gradually, we began to turn the organization around.

It's important to note that when setting individual goals, progress can often be swift, akin to a speedboat. However, when establishing organizational goals, progress can be more deliberate, resembling the gradual course correction of an aircraft carrier. Always keep in mind that progress precedes performance.

Absolutely, it's essential to maintain a well-organized list of your goals and plans. Here are a few key principles to keep in mind:

1. *Make Your List*: Start by creating a comprehensive list of your goals, whether they're personal or organizational. This serves as your roadmap.

2. *Check It Twice*: Regularly review and revise your list to ensure it remains relevant. Check off completed items and update as needed.

3. *Measure Twice and Cut Once*: Before making major decisions or taking significant actions, gather as much information and insight as possible. This prevents costly mistakes.

4. *Keep the Main Thing the Main Thing*: Stay focused on your primary objectives. Don't let distractions or short-term gains divert you from your long-term goals.

5. *Patience is Key*: Understand that progress, whether personal or organizational, often takes time. Be patient and persistent in working toward your goals.

6. *Stay the Course*: As opportunities and challenges arise, use your list and plans to guide your decisions and actions. Don't deviate from your chosen path unless it aligns with your long-term objectives.

7. *Build Your Dynasty*: Consistency and dedication in pursuing your goals will help you establish a legacy of success, whether in your personal life or within your organization.

By adhering to these principles, you can effectively manage your goals and plans, maintaining a steady course toward success.

R.E.A.L. TALK

❖ When it comes to achieving your goals, what are you passionate about?

_____

_____

_____

❖ What constraints are keeping you from achieving your goals?

_____

_____

_____

❖ How comfortable are you in setting goals and conducting strategic plans for an organization?

_____

_____

_____

❖ Is your personal passion and your organizational goals aligned?

_____

_____

_____

★ *Reality: Fulfilling your passion and achieving personal and organizational goals not only brings purpose and satisfaction to your life but also drives innovation and success, ultimately propelling both individual and collective growth.*

CHAPTER 7

Mentor and a Real Influencer

"The greatest good you can do for another is not just to share your riches, but to reveal to them their own." — Benjamin Disraeli

The concept of influence and influencers has indeed taken on new dimensions in the age of social media. It's essential to differentiate between authentic mentors and influencers who genuinely seek your success and those who may be driven solely by personal gain.

1. **Authentic Mentors**: These are individuals who have your best interests at heart and are willing to guide and support you in your personal and professional growth. Authentic mentors invest time and effort in helping you succeed.

2. **Social Media Influencers**: While some social media influencers offer valuable insights and content, it's crucial to scrutinize their motivations and authenticity. Not all influencers are genuinely interested in their followers' well-being; some prioritize personal gain.

3. **Educational Influencers (EIs) and Leadership Influencers (LIs)**: Aspiring to become an Educational Influencer or Leadership Influencer with the goal of positively impacting others is

commendable. True influencers in these domains focus on imparting knowledge, guidance, wisdom, and mentorship to foster growth and success.

When seeking mentors or influencers, consider the following:

- *Alignment with Your Goals*: Ensure that the mentor's or influencer's values and expertise align with your personal and professional objectives.

- *Authenticity*: Look for individuals who genuinely care about your growth and well-being rather than those solely seeking personal gain.

- *Reputation*: Assess their reputation and track record in their respective fields.

- *Accessibility*: Consider how accessible and available they are for guidance and support.

- *Reciprocity*: Be open to offering something in return, such as your dedication and willingness to learn and grow.

Remember that mentors and influencers can play a vital role in your personal and professional development. Choose wisely and build meaningful relationships with those who are invested in your success.

Now, let's take a moment to revisit Chapter One, titled "The Foundation." In this chapter, I recounted some of my life experiences and how they have contributed to shaping my identity. Specifically, I shared a story with you entitled "The Name," exploring the origins of my name. Now, let's leap forward in time, three decades later.

As I contemplated the prospect of leaving my initial post-college job at the state school for special needs students, much like Christopher, I found myself contemplating a transition to the public school system, "yes or no." This change would not only bring me closer to my hometown and my parents but also align with my career goals. During a conversation with my father about my aspirations, he recommended that I reach out to Maurice English, a school administrator and superintendent at Hillsboro ISD in Texas. My dad's recommendation was based on the fact that Maurice was not only a good person but also an alumnus of Frost, the same school from which I had graduated and where my parents had worked.

At my earliest opportunity, I visited the district office to meet and interview with Mr. English. In our introduction, I made sure to mention who my mom and dad were. This initial meeting led to an offer for a teaching position in elementary schools, with the added promise of mentorship to guide my journey toward becoming an administrator. Over the course of the next two years under Maurice's mentorship, I transitioned from an ESL/migrant teacher responsible for two elementary campuses to taking on an assistant role alongside Principal Harvey Wilson, managing these same campuses.

During this period, the district's leadership was undergoing a reorganization, and I was invited to meet with Maurice to discuss my future role. I had spent enough time around Maurice to have a sense of his thinking, and I had anticipated being appointed as the principal of those two elementary schools since Mr. Wilson, the current principal, was moving into a central office role as the assistant superintendent.

I vividly recall sitting across from Maurice at his desk, feeling somewhat anxious about what was to come. However, when he informed me of his decision, it caught me completely off guard. He expressed his desire for me to become the assistant principal at Hillsboro High School. At that very moment, I experienced a surge of surprise and uncertainty, as if Maurice had thrown me an unexpected and somewhat intimidating curveball—a feeling akin to trying to decipher one of his legendary baseball pitches.

No matter which metaphor I employ, the relationship I had with Maurice opened doors and provided opportunities that propelled me to levels I had never before envisioned. I had always aspired to be a professional basketball player, and when that dream didn't materialize, I shifted my focus to becoming a teacher and coach. The idea of becoming a school administrator had never even crossed my mind. Little did I know that my introduction to high school administration in Hillsboro ISD, specifically at Hillsboro High School in 1983, would mark the beginning of my administrative career.

Just two years after our initial meeting in 1985, Maurice recommended me to the school board, and they approved my appointment as the principal of Hillsboro High School. At that time, I was a 29-year-old African-American man sporting a jerry curl hairstyle! Throughout this journey, Maurice and Harvey continued to serve as my mentors in the field of educational leadership. They generously shared their wisdom and knowledge, drawing from their illustrious careers, and displayed a genuine desire to see me succeed in mine.

Maurice's mentorship extended beyond the professional realm. He organized yearly trips for me and my assistant principal, Don Rinehart, which encompassed a mix of work-related events and leisure activities aimed at helping us strike a healthy work-life balance. Remarkably, he never intruded on my religious beliefs or tried to lecture me about faith. Instead, he exemplified the qualities of a divine leader, sharing his wisdom, leadership experiences, and theories through tangible examples. He effectively embodied all the leadership traits I've discussed. During the Christmas season, I could always count on him to gift me the latest edition of the Upper Room for my personal reading enjoyment.

Maurice was not just an exceptional mentor; he and his wife, Ginger, hold a special place in my heart and in the hearts of my family. I will forever be grateful to Maurice for recognizing the potential within me even before I had a glimpse of it myself. I had the honor of speaking at Maurice's retirement receptions, marking the first time I publicly shared the profound impact of Maurice's leadership, mentorship, and enduring friendship.

During these speeches, I encouraged the audience to reflect on the pivotal moment when Maurice English, in his capacity as superintendent of Hillsboro ISD, made the bold recommendation to the Board of Trustees to appoint me as the high school principal at the tender age of 29. This appointment not only marked a significant milestone in my career but also established me as the first African-American to hold that position in Hillsboro ISD's history.

I urged the audience to contemplate the formidable nature of the decision Maurice had to make. I acknowledged that he peered beyond the color of my skin and recognized in me the potential to excel in the role. This showcased his embodiment of the leadership trait "courage." Indeed, it takes immense courage to make tough and unconventional decisions. From Maurice, I gleaned the invaluable lesson that one must resolutely stand by their convictions.

I recounted being present at the board meeting that night, where the executive session spanned several hours before they emerged to cast their votes in favor of Maurice's recommendation. He never explicitly divulged the specifics of that executive session; however, he did mention that the board president, Dr. John Erwin, unwaveringly supported his recommendation and exerted significant "influence" during the meeting. Considering the courage displayed by these respected individuals within the community and their professions to provide me with an opportunity in a predominantly white school underscored the magnitude of this decision.

We also had the privilege of nurturing some exceptional students, many of whom I still maintain contact with to this day. Witnessing the quality education and remarkable accomplishments these students attained at

Hillsboro High School filled me with immense pride. Our school boasted outstanding students, dedicated parents, and an unwavering competitive spirit in every arena we participated in—spanning academics, athletics, band, one-act plays, debate, and vocational competitions. Throughout my tenure of seven years as the high school principal, the student's achievements, both in academics and extracurricular activities, were notably significant. Dr. Erwin recently conveyed that what the administration, teachers, coaches, and staff achieved during this period could be likened to a "Mountain Top Experience." His influence continues to resonate.

This serves as a compelling illustration of how mentors and influential figures can profoundly shape your life and career. Moreover, it underscores the significant role that "experience and timing" play in one's life. It's worth recalling the actions of my dad three decades earlier during the game where I received my name. His commitment to engaging with students during a period of racial unrest in society (notably, Emmett Till's murder on August 28, 1955) demonstrated his courage and dedication to the young men under his care. Maurice English, who was a student on that bus, undoubtedly benefited from such leadership.

R.E.A.L. TALK

❖ Have you ever had someone throw you a wicked curveball that had a positive or negative impact on your career?

_____

_____

_____

❖ What do you believe is the difference between a mentor and an influencer? How do you see them impacting your life and career?

_____

_____

_____

❖ How has a relationship or timing impacted your career?

_____

_____

_____

❖ Did anyone see the potential in you before you realized it was there?

_____

_____

_____

❖ Have you or your organization had a "Mountain Top Experience"?

_____

_____

_____

★ *Reality: The strategic alignment of timing and nurturing relationships can significantly shape and advance your career, opening doors of opportunity and accelerating professional success.*

CHAPTER 8

Survivor

(Diversity Overcomes Adversity)

"Out of many, we are one. That while we breathe, we hope. And when we are met with cynicism and doubts and those who tell us that we can't, we will respond with that timeless creed that sums up the spirit of a people: Yes, we can!" — Barack Obama

I had the privilege of serving as the superintendent for the La Marque Independent School District and witnessed the zenith of academic excellence and outstanding achievements in numerous co-curricular and extracurricular domains, including basketball, track and field, band, and football, among others.

Dr. Mike Moses, former Commissioner of the Texas Education Agency, once wrote a reference letter for me;

> *"It has been my privilege to know Dr. Johnson for the last twenty years. During the time that I have known him, he has compiled an outstanding record of successful school leadership in the state of Texas. He has served in all positions in public schools, having worked as an elementary teacher, assistant principal, high school principal, field service agent, assistant superintendent, and*

superintendent in three Texas school districts. He also served as the Associate Commissioner of Education for the Texas Education Agency from 2006-2008.

To say that Dr. Johnson has touched "all the bases" would be an understatement. He has achieved success and distinction in all the positions in which he has served.

From 1995-1989, I served as superintendent of schools in the La Marque Independent School District. Dr. Johnson served in that same position from 2001-2006. From my acquaintances and knowledge of the La Marque District, I am most familiar with the great success that he achieved while working in that district. He built community support and led the district to unparalleled accomplishments in terms of student achievement and extracurricular activities..."

Work Ethic

While I was relaxing in my recliner, my phone rang. It displayed the name Bryan Erwin, who served as both the athletic director and head football coach in La Marque ISD. It was a typical Thursday call, as he would keep me updated on the athletic program, especially regarding the preparations for the upcoming football game. I would often inquire, "Is the hay in the barn?"

Mr. Bernard Porter

This expression stemmed from my experiences growing up, working on farms and hauling hay with family and friends. It was ingrained in us as a work ethic: the job isn't done until all the bales of hay are collected from the field, properly loaded onto the truck to prevent loss, driven to the barn, unloaded into the barn, and the barn door is securely closed. Mr. Porter, the ranch owner, would always ask at the end of the day, "Is the hay in the barn?"

It took a diverse team to accomplish this task. We had distinct roles within our team, including drivers, loaders, stackers, and, upon reaching the barn, unloaders and additional stackers to ensure all the hay made it inside. Surviving the demanding work, scorching heat, and dusty conditions was undeniably challenging. Nonetheless, our diverse and cohesive team allowed us to overcome numerous obstacles, and we found considerable success in our hay-hauling endeavors. There was a unique inspiration among this group of hay haulers that forged a lasting bond, enduring to this day. Our collective determination helped us navigate not only the taxing conditions, such as scorching heat and the potential presence of poisonous snakes in the fields and barns but also the sheer physical demands of the work. Remarkably, everyone on our hay hauling team, along with their siblings who weren't part of the hay crew, managed to complete high school, attend college, and achieve successful careers in fields like agriculture, business, dentistry, education, and law. The job was only considered finished when the hay was safely stored in the barn.

Coach Erwin understood the significance I placed on developing a strong work ethic and the importance of thorough preparation, firmly believing that "luck is what happens when preparation meets opportunity." The La Marque Independent School District (ISD) provided an exceptional opportunity to showcase the remarkable talents of our students and student-athletes.

La Marque ISD boasted a rich tradition both academically and athletically, with the football team having made six appearances in the state finals and clinched three state championships prior to my arrival. However, their last championship victory dates back to the late '80s.

I had recruited Bryan from Hillsboro High School, where he had been coaching and where I had previously served as the high school principal. Bryan was one of Dr. John and Martha Erwin's sons. Martha, a professional nurse, was also a dedicated mother, specializing in supporting her sons and all the students of Hillsboro High School. Bryan had three other brothers who had all made their family and community immensely proud with their service and success in life. Dr. John Erwin pursued a career in the medical field, Mark Erwin became an entrepreneur, and Brent, also in the medical field, played a pivotal role on the frontlines during the recent coronavirus pandemic. It's truly an extraordinary family. You should also know that Bryan and Steve Hale, his defensive coordinator, and all of his brothers were students while I was an administrator at Hillsboro High School.

Bryan's interview was one of the most impressive I've ever witnessed from a candidate. To select the right candidate for this position, we assembled a committee, recognizing that this role generated more attention than hiring a superintendent. Among the candidates were remarkable individuals who had coached alongside the legendary Coach Waddell during La Marque's six consecutive appearances in the State finals in football, along with other seasoned candidates from across the state. However, Bryan stood out as my choice due to his exceptional interview and the passion I believed he would infuse into the program.

He had gone to great lengths in his preparation, conducting research on each member of the committee. Bryan presented each of us with personalized notebooks outlining his comprehensive plan for the program, with a particular emphasis on nurturing character development in young boys and girls, helping them transition into responsible young men and women. What impressed me most, though, was his heartfelt connection to the school, as he had memorized the school song. Throughout the interview, at perfectly timed moments, he recited stanzas from the school song, underscoring the significance of "the Blue, the Gold, and the White."

Once my decision to recommend Coach Bryan Erwin went public, a slew of malicious rumors began circulating. One that stands out is the false claim that Dr. Erwin had operated on my dad, which was the reason behind my decision (my dad was not even a patient of Dr. Erwin). I was even labeled an "Uncle Tom" by some because I hadn't hired an African-American. However, in line with the principles I had learned from my mentor, Maurice English, I stood firm in my convictions despite the easier paths I could have taken. I demonstrated the leadership trait of courage, just as I had witnessed in others.

While easier options existed, such as hiring one of the former assistants from the championship program or selecting an African-American candidate, I firmly believed in my heart and soul that this decision was in the best interest of the student-athletes. With the support of board members Dr. Bill Spillar and Mr. Frank Proctor, the board backed my recommendation. When we emerged from the executive session with the votes to pass the motion, we were in for a surprise. A junior student-athlete named Rashad Bobino had taken my seat and was holding the board gavel. We allowed him to call the meeting to order, and the board moved forward with the motion, hiring Bryan Erwin as the Athletic Director and Head Football Coach. Mr. Bobino also declared, from the diocese, that La Marque High School would become an exemplary academic institution, and we were destined to win a state championship.

Upon Coach Erwin's appointment, I witnessed how he swiftly began shaping and instilling a strong set of beliefs in both students and staff. He took charge of every situation and room he entered, leaving a profound impact. I remember one occasion when I visited his office and noticed he was soaking wet. My initial assumption was that the players had tossed him into the swimming pool. I thought to myself, *Come on, Coach! You can't let the students play pranks like that on you!* However, he later clarified that he was drenched in perspiration from working out with the team, a dedication that reminded me of our days in the hay field. This demonstrated his commitment to doing everything he asked of his students, serving as a true servant leader.

Throughout my career, I have seen numerous coaches treat their teams as mere workers, and there's nothing inherently wrong with this approach as long as the players understand the coach's genuine intentions. Rigorous training is essential to achieving success, but it must be paired with unconditional love and respect.

Now, let's dive into the diversity aspect. Coach Erwin had informed me that we had an exceptionally talented group of players across all positions, including linemen, defensive backs, quarterback, linebackers, running backs, and receivers. However, there was one position where we had a gap—a placekicker. Coach ventured over to the soccer field and noticed a freshman who showed potential, convincing him to become the La Marque Cougars' placekicker. This young man was so slim and tiny that they had to tape his football pants to prevent them from slipping when he kicked. His initial extra-point attempt hit the center in the rear! Nevertheless, he persevered and didn't give up.

Despite the fact that our team was predominantly African-American, Coach Erwin successfully built a diverse team, both in terms of ethnicity and in their shared commitment to their goals. We encountered adversity from various sources, including community members who desired an African-American coach, challenges from neighboring districts and the UIL regarding eligibility, and one of the toughest schedules in Class 4A football. The courage I displayed began to pay off, as evidenced by the team's unexpected journey to the regional finals in our first year in La Marque, despite predictions that we wouldn't even make the playoffs.

When I picked up the phone, it was clear that Coach Erwin was brimming with excitement. However, it wasn't about the usual football preparation talk, known as "the hay being in the barn." Instead, he was eager to share a book he had introduced to his football team and coaches. The book in question was *A Purpose Driven Life* by Rick Warren, which delved into the significance of the number "40" and its numerous references in the Bible. He mentioned that his local pastor had delivered a sermon about the book on the preceding Sunday and was so moved by it that he felt compelled to share it with the team.

During that phone call, Bryan said, "Dr. J, you won't believe this! I purchased a copy of this book for each team member, and tonight, after practice, we conducted our very first book study. Considering the biblical significance of the number 40, we realized that if we read one chapter a day, we would finish all forty chapters in the book on the fortieth day—the same day we would be playing for the state championship!"

I won't delve into the entire story of the La Marque Cougars' remarkable title run, where they achieved a perfect 16-0 record and clinched the state championship in 2003. I'll leave the details of that extraordinary journey to be shared by the coaches, players, and devoted Cougar fans. However, I will share the pivotal conclusion of this story, so consider this a spoiler alert.

On that fortieth night from the phone call I described earlier, the coach and his team faced adversity from the moment he took charge until that unforgettable night. I had the privilege of witnessing what a coach of faith, leading a diverse team, can accomplish against all odds, particularly in a triple-overtime game. In this intense matchup, the place kicker found himself in the spotlight, having to make not one but two critical extra-point kicks from 30 yards out due to penalties. These kicks were essential to keep the Cougars' hopes of securing another state championship alive.

It's worth noting that this game featured numerous exceptional players and coaches, with a significant number of them going on to become Division I athletes and enjoying illustrious college careers. Many, including myself, consider this contest to be one of the greatest games in the history of high school playoffs. However, that narrative belongs to them, while my point is this:

Maurice English

Much like Maurice English, who displayed the courage to make tough decisions, it is crucial to understand the importance of diversity, especially when facing adversity. Developing a strong work ethic that ensures tasks are completed, combined with the positive influence of individuals like Dr. John Erwin Jr., reinforces my belief that diversity will triumph over adversity every time. It's yet another "Mountain Top Experience" that vividly illustrates the power of unwavering faith and determination.

Just see it!

R.E.A.L. TALK

❖ Describe a time when you showed courage when making a tough decision.

❖ When you think of diversity, what comes to your mind?

❖ How have you faced adversity in your career so far? Were you successful, and why or why not?

❖ How would you describe a diverse team in your organization? What would it look like?

❖ Share a "Mountain Top Experience" from your life and/or career.

_____

_____

_____

★ *Reality: Diversity harnesses a wealth of perspectives, experiences, and strengths, enabling a collective resilience that triumphs over adversity and fuels progress toward achieving goals.*

Conclusion

I chose the title *Reality Leadership 2.0* with a profound desire to offer something beyond the usual theories, leadership styles, and countless leadership models that are crucial components of leadership training. I aimed to provide you with genuine, real-life leadership experiences that establish a tangible connection with the world of work, along with a touch of entertainment and intrigue. Over the years, I've delivered speeches and presentations, and what people tend to remember most are the stories I shared: "The Trail," "The Name," and "The Tale of the Purple Hull Peas." I believe the reason these stories resonate is their authenticity. They aren't based on fanciful dreams I had on a subway ride or how I miraculously saved a fictitious Fortune 500 company from bankruptcy. By sharing real leadership experiences, we can examine leadership traits within tangible scenarios, enabling us to immediately relate these leadership principles and concepts to Relevant Executive Administrative Leadership (R.E.A.L.) experiences.

As we explore these stories, we can pose pertinent questions for ourselves and others. While there are excellent books that outline effective leadership models and provide comprehensive plans for becoming successful leaders, I personally view them as tools in my toolbox to be used if the need arises. To be candid, it's essential to refrain from dictating what I should do when the advice comes from individuals lacking experience in my field. If someone assumes a leadership role over leaders in a domain they've never worked in, it amounts to mere talk or suggestions. Similarly, if someone leads in a profession they've never previously been part of, and no one is following their lead, it's akin to just walking. Effective leaders must possess firsthand experience in the field they have been chosen, elevated, appointed, or selected to lead. A wise friend once reminded me that even if I hold the title "Dr. Johnson," it doesn't qualify me to be appointed as the Surgeon General!

Nonetheless, I firmly believe that a leadership book, authored from the perspective of an educational leader, replete with authentic, contemporary life and leadership examples, has a place in the toolbox of various industries and companies. Leadership, in my view, transcends industry boundaries. Whether it's a Fortune 500 Corporation or a family-owned business, leadership shares a common foundation rooted in experiences that are universally applicable across industries. The field of education, in particular, represents an extreme form of human service, and our commonality lies in our dealings with diverse people and our capacity to adapt to a multitude of situations. In the realm of human service, we must excel at providing exceptional customer service and delivering crucial conversations when needed.

Stress is an inherent facet of the human service industry because our success or failure hinges on our ability to effectively engage and understand people. We must acknowledge that, fundamentally, we share more similarities than differences. Consequently, I believe that a one-size-fits-all approach cannot be applied to working with leaders. We each possess our unique DNA (deoxyribonucleic acid), individual leadership skills, and life experiences. Exceptional leaders must be adept at customizing, modifying, and adapting to the prevailing circumstances. Whether it entails making an emergency water landing or safely landing an aircraft without landing gear, leaders must be prepared for any situation. Whether it involves opting for the path of least resistance to secure a promotion or embracing a more challenging route while enduring criticism because it aligns with one's principles, sometimes the right choice entails taking the less-traveled path.

It is imperative to nurture a diverse repertoire of leadership traits and skills capable of accommodating the distinctive needs of various stakeholders, including customers, clients, stakeholders, colleagues, staff, and boards of directors, to become adaptable leaders. Each of these stakeholders possesses unique DKA (Desires, Knowledge, Attitudes) shaped by their life experiences and narratives. By sharing and timing these narratives, individuals can become more attuned to their own experiences and better equipped to lead effectively.

Reflecting back to 1955, when a bus driver's experience led to my own journey, I aim to share my accumulated wisdom in mentoring and training future leaders.

Instead of a one-size-fits-all approach, I advocate for rigorous, personalized training that respects each individual's unique story and experiences, emphasizing observation and practical scenarios, such as landing a plane on water or handling challenging situations, as key components to develop effective leaders.

Given the rise of reality television, now is an opportune moment to introduce a "reality leadership" perspective that can better equip leaders to navigate real-life situations. Motivated by my wife, who works in human resources and witnesses the costly consequences of unprepared leaders, I've been inspired to write this book and provide the training needed to address these critical leadership gaps.

I remember her sharing a story with me not too long ago. She really believed that she needed additional staff because the department is bombarded with unexpected situations that occur daily and weekly. During budget development for the next fiscal year, each department was asked to present its staffing needs. She was receiving pushback from her supervisors and the financial managers that she didn't need any additional staff. While she was making her case to the executive team, her phone rang during the middle of her presentation. She looked at the caller ID and said to the team, "Excuse me, but I need to take this call from a campus administrator. Hello?"

Then there was a long pause, and then she said, "When did this happen? Have you taken their statements? No? Okay, we will do that. I would try to find someone to get to your campus as soon as possible, but my only investigator is conducting interviews on another case at this time. So, keep the individuals involved in this instance isolated, and I will get there as soon as I finish my meeting with the executive team about staffing for next year. If you are contacted by the media, please refer them to our Public Relations Department. No worries. Thank you for calling. You're following proper procedures." Click. She hangs up.

The executive team was anxious to learn what the problem was, and she shared with them that this was a staged example of how a human resource office has to be prepared every day for real organizational situations.

Her compelling real-life experience during the executive team meeting, where she adeptly handled a pressing issue while making her case for additional staffing, served as a powerful illustration of the constant need for readiness in human resources to address unforeseen organizational challenges and situations, ultimately leading to the approval of her staffing request.

As the author of this book, I've engaged in countless discussions with education officials at various levels, administrators, and staff, delving into the vast array of books, policies, and programs designed to enhance student outcomes and the overall quality of education. Through these conversations, it's become evident that the key lessons for administrators and executives center around the importance of bringing reality leadership to the forefront, offering rigorous training for future leaders, and providing executive coaching to equip them with the necessary skills to address both daily challenges and unexpected issues that arise continuously. In recognizing that missions and visions are only valuable when executed, my aim is to nurture leaders capable of executing the mission and vision effectively, regardless of the circumstances they encounter.

Finally, while reflecting on the bond between father and son, it's clear that my dad's wisdom and guidance deeply influenced my upbringing. As evidenced by his heartfelt words, my character is a testament to the values instilled in me.

In a 2005 article from the Corsicana Daily Sun, written by Chris Smith, my dad said he was proud of me. Smith drew parallels between my father's and my relationship and the divine affirmation given to Jesus, indicating that our connection transcends mere blood ties—it is a bond built on respect, admiration, and a shared legacy of warmth and strength. In the article, Smith writes that my dad stated, *"When God was speaking to Jesus, He said, 'This is my beloved Son, in whom I am well pleased.' Adrian is my only son, and I am well pleased with him."*

Smith continued to write, *"Johnson is proud of the way he raised his son, who understands that his dad is still the boss. Adrian undoubtedly inherited his strong character from his father, whose warm, laid-back personality captivates those around him through the stories he shares."*

R.E.A.L. TALK

- ❖ What about you? How did you arrive at this page?

  _____
  _____
  _____

- ❖ What do you believe about leadership?

  _____
  _____
  _____

- ❖ Is it based on reality or something else?

  _____
  _____
  _____

- ❖ How will your beliefs serve you?

  _____
  _____
  _____

★ *Reality: My beliefs, experiences, journey, and story shape my reality as a leader by providing the foundation of values, resilience, and wisdom that guide my decision-making and inspire others to follow. What's your reality?*

THANK YOU FOR READING MY BOOK!

Thank you for buying and reading my book! My hope is that this has encouraged you to become the leader that you were destined to be.

To connect with me, please scan the QR Code below:

I appreciate your interest in my book and value your feedback as it helps me improve future versions. I would appreciate it if you could leave your invaluable review on Amazon.com with your feedback. Thank you!

www.ingramcontent.com/pod-product-compliance
Lightning Source LLC
Chambersburg PA
CBHW061650040426
42446CB00010B/1666